You are the Answer

Why it's time to trust your body

Naomi Mills

Chiropractor

ISBN 978-1-8384188-1-6
Published in 2021 by Biddles UK Ltd.

The views expressed in this book are those of the author. The author of this book does not dispense medical advice or prescribe the use of any technique as a form of treatment for physical, emotional or medical problems without the seeking advice from your healthcare provider. The intent of the author is only to offer general information and personal to help you in your quest for physical, emotional and spiritual wellbeing. In the event that you use any of the information contained in this book, you do so at your own risk.

For Richard and Beatrix and
everyone who is open to creating
more joy in their lives.

Contents

Preface

It's 4pm on Tuesday 8 December 2015 and I'm sitting on my sofa beside a twinkling Christmas tree, put up 2 weeks earlier than usual so that I can enjoy its soft glow during my planned home birth. My 10-day-old daughter Beatrix lies asleep on my chest after a feed. I feel exhausted and slightly detached from myself. I assume this is how every mother who has just given birth feels, it's my first time so I wouldn't know. My brain doesn't remind me of the many women I have seen over the years who have arrived to their scheduled Chiropractic appointment with me and proudly presented me with a baby they have given birth to the day, or even evening before. I have forgotten that not everybody feels as though they have been run over by a bus following childbirth.

My phone rings and it's my independent midwife who has been out to see us that morning as part of her daily check-ins. Today she commented on how tired I seemed and noticed I was slightly breathless when changing my bedsheets. "I've been thinking about you all day," she tells me, "something doesn't feel right. I've spoken to your GP and he is going to see you at the surgery in an hour, just to put my mind at rest." My husband, Beatrix and I head down to the GP expecting a quick visit. He is very careful in his examination, which includes measuring the circumference around each of my calf muscles. One is 2cm larger than the other but as a Chiropractor, I know that all bodies are different. "It could be normal variation", I tell him. He agrees with me, but acting on his own instinct he wants me to have a blood test at the hospital just to be safe.

At the hospital, the junior doctor assures us that once the results of the blood tests come back, we will be heading home. I don't have any 'significant' symptoms, it's just routine. The results take a while, so Beatrix and I are taken to the post-natal ward to wait and my husband goes home. At 3am I am awoken by a huddle of doctors around my bed. They want me to have a chest CT which, they tell me, will increase my lifetime risk of developing breast cancer by 10%. I don't want to have the scan if I don't absolutely need it, I don't want to do anything that makes me more likely to have cancer and I tell them so. "You have to be alive to have breast cancer" the female doctor replies.

My blood results showed my heart was breaking down into my blood and they didn't know why. The consultant radiographer who was called into the hospital at 4am to do my scan even commented, "If this woman has a blood clot, I'll give £5000 to charity." The scan revealed I had 2 clots blocking my heart. Pulmonary embolism is one of the biggest killers of post-natal women in the UK with 66% of new mothers dying within 30 minutes of a clot forming. Despite being young and healthy and having had a home water birth, I had won a form of healthy lottery, becoming that rare person that develops a clot in the days after giving birth. Given the wrong set of circumstances, even healthy bodies can become seriously sick.

When I first got my medical diagnosis of 'bilateral pulmonary emboli' I expected an equally medical solution. Surely the doctors had developed some sort of laser to break them down, or a drug that would dissolve it? Not so. All that could be done was to thin my blood to prevent more blood cells from sticking to the clot to make it bigger, like snowflakes creating a snowball. Otherwise, the solution was to give my body rest and time to break down the clots on its own. Rest and time to heal, the two most common pieces of advice I gave my clients every day. Here I was in a life-threatening situation and I had to trust my body to save me.

I am so thankful that my background as a Chiropractor meant that I already trusted the natural cleverness of my body and so I was able to accept this plan of action and feel at peace with it. I gladly accepted the blood thinners so that my body didn't have to work as hard to get the job done. Within a few months, the clots had broken down and I was able to make a full recovery, thanks to the fact my body knew what to do in a crisis, just as it had in childbirth. Medicine is most valuable when it supports the natural processes of our bodies or when it can rescue us when mother nature cannot. However, it is not in our best interest to look only to medicine to maintain our health. Your body has a natural cleverness and healing power all of its own. By trusting in your body, you can have faith in your ability to play a part in your own healing process. May you never underestimate how important that is.

I've spent the last 20 years of my life caring for people: half in care homes and hospitals, half as a Chiropractor and it saddens me how little interaction there is between medicine and natural healthcare.

Our current system, based on the idea that the human body is in its essence weak and vulnerable, is wrong. It ignores the natural cleverness which runs through our nervous system, giving us the ability to heal, adapt and create resilience to stress and ill health. By understanding and working with this system rather than against it, each of us can learn to trust our body and create our own health.

Medicine and surgery have a place, but only where Mother Nature needs support and for all our sakes, should never be the first or only step. My vision is for a world that promotes good health, over managing sickness. By honouring the awesome partnership of body and brain through the central nervous system, we can find hundreds of ways to create a long and happy life. For this to happen we need to look inside ourselves for the answer. The first step is to reconnect with our natural cleverness, learn to trust the signals our bodies give us and interpret them into action.

This book is intended to show how and why shifting our reliance for health away from external resources and back inside each person, is the most rewarding and reliable way to create lasting health and happiness for our whole community.

HEALTH KEY

By trusting in your body, you can have faith in your ability to play a part in your own healing process

Introduction

Growing up I always knew that I wanted a job where I could help people. In my eight-year-old brain, 'helping people' meant helping them to feel good in their own skin. I was also very interested in the human body and my favourite book for many years was *Blood, Bones and Body Bits*. Every tiny, disgusting and amazing fact I learned only made me more curious to understand how human-beings work. Because of this, I naturally assumed I would become a medical doctor. After all, what other job would allow me to talk to people all day and work with human bodies? Doctor had to be the job for me.

Because I like to test theories before putting them into practice, I decided to do a year of work experience in a hospital before I started a medical degree. At 18 I got a job as an assistant nurse in a surgical ward at a busy hospital. Life at the hospital was hard for the people working there. Everyone had to work to their maximum capacity most of the time, and the politics and power structures meant there wasn't much flexibility in the job. Even though staff cared about patients a lot, they were rarely able to go above and beyond for them or build relationships. Instead, many of my colleagues were stressed and worn down from years of caring for others. It took all of their energy just to get through each day and it was easy to see how, after a few years, my own enthusiasm and drive would also be diminished.

It also bothered me that after their surgery, patients were sent home 'as soon as they were (medically) ready' but often this was before that person was emotionally prepared or physically strong. As a care assistant, patients would often share these fears with me, knowing they didn't have the extra support they needed at home. I remember one woman was so desperate to stay in hospital where she felt safe and supported, that after being discharged from the ward she sat in the main reception until I found her later that day.

My time at the hospital showed me that while I still really wanted to help people, this particular way of helping didn't seem to fit me. I loved the work, and I liked my colleagues, but something didn't feel quite right. The jobs I saw the doctors and nurses doing didn't look anything like the ideal job I had in my head.

It would take nearly 15 years for me to be able to understand why this traditional model of healthcare and helping didn't fit me perfectly. Over this time, I have gone on a huge journey both personally and professionally. I have come to understand that the human body is incredibly clever and that when we honour this cleverness and work with it, everyone can experience more energy, health and joy in their life. You don't need a medical degree to understand how your body works. You just need a body!

Most doctors will tell you that their training is almost exclusively about when things go wrong with the body, with very little time to spare on how it is naturally clever and designed to heal on its own. If medicine focuses on everything which can go wrong for you, I have written this book to remind you of everything that is already right within you. By knowing this for yourself, you can take back control of your health.

Everything I've learned can be summarised by these 4 core beliefs:

- The whole capacity of the human body, how it works as a system, is much greater than the sum of its parts
- Health comes from the inside out, not the outside in
- The human body has a natural cleverness, in other words symptoms happen for a reason
- Being healthy means enjoying a friendly relationship with my body where I know I can trust and rely on it.

In this book I want to share my journey: the experiences, people, challenges and realisations that helped form these beliefs. I also want to share how they have helped me to make more sense of my health and the world around me and in doing so, completely transformed my life. There is so much that I want to share with you in the hope that it does the same for you.

Chapter 1 is all about my favourite topic: your clever body. It's so important that you realise up front, that you are not broken or flawed, but already have everything within you to live an awesome, healthy and fulfilling life.

In Chapter 2, I will explore ideas around health and encourage you to gently question some of your pre-conceived beliefs around what health looks like and what it really means to be healthy.

This is essential before going on to Chapter 3 where we explore your life potential. This is the part where you start to take control of your health and future happiness. Where you can look beyond today, into how you want to experience life in the future. When you can see how clever you naturally are, and that health isn't just about 'not being sick' but about enjoying a complete sense of wellbeing, a world of possibilities will open up for you.

Finally, in Chapter 4 I share all the practical tools and tips that have helped me on my journey up to this point. After reading this book, I don't want you to rely on anyone for your health and happiness other than yourself. Of course, you'll always benefit from the help and support of friends and professionals. But you are the decision maker. You know what is best for you, because you understand why it is so important to be connected to your body, how to hear and understand its signals and what action to take next.

A lot of the ideas I explore in this book are based on the latest science and research, particularly in the field of neuroscience (the study of how the brain affects the body through the nervous system). To keep this book light and easy to read, I have stuck with the broad brush-strokes of some complex scientific ideas. If you have a need to understand a particular concept on a more detailed level, I encourage you to explore this for yourself.

Working with the natural cleverness of your body will change your life. Your body is clever because your brain and body work in partnership. Re-connecting your brain to the inner world of your body creates a tremendous shift on the inside which is reflected on your outside. Seeing this shift happen for people, when they become re-connected to their inner world, is the most rewarding job I can imagine. I see it every day in my work as a Chiropractor and I hope that after reading this book, you will begin the process of making your body a friendlier place to be. It's important to do, since the two of you (your brain and body) are together for a lifetime. The quality of that life is directly made better or worse, depending on how well your body-brain partnership is working.

If you're ready, let's get started!

HEALTH KEY

Your body's ability to heal is much greater than anyone has allowed you to believe

Chapter 1: How Your Clever Body Works

I will always remember the first time my daughter had a proper fever. She was 18 months old and instead of being her bubbly, running-around self, she was hot, had no energy and was generally miserable. Of course, my first instinct as a parent was to take the hurt away. I wanted to make her feel better, so she didn't suffer more than she had to. My husband suggested giving her medicine to relieve the fever, but I didn't want her to have it. I prefer to do things naturally and knew that by giving her medicine, Beatrix would be up and running around again too quickly. I thought that giving her a false feeling of 'better' would ultimately prolong her recovery and her discomfort.

Despite this, seeing my little girl miserable and exhausted made it incredibly tempting to give her something to ease the pain. I knew a one-off dose wasn't going to damage her in the long term, so against my better judgement, I gave her some medicine. As expected, she perked up and had a much happier afternoon and for a moment, I was almost happy she took the medicine. Seeing her little face brighten as the discomfort eased was a powerful message to the parent inside me who just wanted to make everything okay again.

However, as the drugs wore off 4 hours later, she was much more exhausted and unhappy than she had been before. Rest was what her body needed to channel all its resources into killing the virus. By lowering her temperature and taking away the pain, I had created the opposite conditions needed for my child to heal. Nature knew exactly what it was doing, and I had overridden that natural cleverness and made things worse. Even though I *knew* I could trust her body, I had been seduced by the promise of a quick fix. I was so mad at myself!

After this, my husband and I honoured what her symptoms were telling us and let her ride it out. Twenty-four hours later she was recovered, zooming around and back at nursery. Her teacher was surprised she was coming back so soon, as "most other children were off a whole week with this one, not just two days."

Nothing has tested my health beliefs more than parenthood. As a Chiropractor, my days are spent appreciating the everyday miracle of the body healing itself. On this day however, I underestimated the cleverness of my young daughter's body, believing that I knew better. I thought something was wrong because her symptoms were uncomfortable. I had forgotten that symptoms happen for a reason. She felt sick and tired because she needed rest. Hot, because a raised temperature will de-activate the virus. Not hungry, because she needed all her energy to fight the virus, not having it used up in digesting her food.

Learning from our mistakes is the most human thing in the world. Now, any time my daughter is unwell, I trust that her body is making her feel how it needs to, to get her to behave in a way that allows her to heal. I am trying to teach her how to hear the signals from her body and to trust and honour them. Through her, nature is teaching me at the same time!

Each time it happens, trusting that the symptoms have a purpose gets easier to do. However, trusting the in-built cleverness of your body is not something most of us are taught to do. If anything, modern healthcare teaches you that your body can't be trusted and that you can't possibly be well without external 'help'. No wonder that letting nature run its course feels counterintuitive.

The realisation that your symptoms happen *for* you and not *to* you, is a game changer: it's the first step towards building a strong and trusting relationship with your body.

HEALTH KEY

Symptoms happen *for* you, not *to* you

What is a 'clever body'?

"Looking for consciousness in the brain is like looking inside your radio for the announcer" Nassim Haramein

---

Having a clever body isn't something we give much thought to, in fact the design of our bodies means we aren't meant to think about it. That's the whole point! I think your body is clever because you were born with millions of mini manuals all uploaded into your brain, so you can do millions of tiny actions at once, without ever having to think about it.

A quick internet search for 'things my body does without me even having to think about it' comes up with:

- Regulating temperature including sweating, hairs standing on end and blood vessels expanding or constricting, depending on what's needed
- Adjusting our balance, blood pressure and oxygen levels in relation to our environment and activity
- Producing, releasing and balancing hormones
- Secreting saliva, tears, stomach juices and other secretions in the lungs, gut, pancreas and gall bladder

- Filtering out toxins from the body and alerting us when urine stores are full
- Blinking, breathing and seeing
- Making, storing and altering memories in the brain
- Selectively filtering out information from the world around you that isn't important right now

I could easily fill the rest of the pages in this book with more examples of how your body is cleverly doing countless complicated things all at once. The more you realise just how much work your body does every day to keep you alive, the easier it is to trust its cleverness. I call this natural cleverness 'innate' or in-built intelligence.

Your natural cleverness is that 'spark' of life that is the difference between a body which is living and one which is not. It can't be seen, or easily measured, weighed or quantified in some way. This is why scientists still argue over exactly when this spark begins at birth or ends at death. However, this mysterious nature doesn't make it any less real or important. Your natural cleverness powers a never-ending cycle where your body collects information from your environment, feeds it to your brain which then organises it, sending new instructions back to the body.

I believe that how this cleverness expresses itself with you is what makes you unique. Although most of us are born with the same body parts and feel related to each other as human beings sharing this planet, none of us express ourselves or experience life in the same way. This is what makes life so exciting. Rather than focussing on trying to explain this spark of cleverness which is inside you, if you can accept that it exists, there's a lot you can gain by exploring just how far it can take you...

> HEALTH KEY
>
> The more you realise how much work your body does every day to keep you alive, the easier it is to trust its cleverness

Your body is clever – trust it

"The single most important decision any of us will ever make is whether or not to believe that the universe is friendly" Albert Einstein

---

It makes me sad every time someone questions whether they are 'up to it' when it comes to achieving something their body was naturally designed for. It could be questioning whether *their* body can become fitter or stronger ("I know other people can have fat in their diet and still loose weight, but will it work for me?"). It might be someone who doesn't believe they can recover from an injured disc in their spine without painkillers and believes deep down that a fusion surgery is inevitable. When you do not have an underlying trust in your body, it is hard to believe that you can achieve difficult things. By working with your body and not against it, you can discover just how clever and adaptable your body has evolved to be.

For me, nothing in this world represents the amazing intelligence of the human body more than pregnancy. The fact that a single sperm and egg combined, contain all the information they need to grow a full human body: brain, organs, tissue, bones, teeth, hair and everything else, is mind blowing. Being pregnant is one of the biggest tests of how much trust you have in the natural cleverness of your body. Even if you have never been pregnant yourself, when you think about someone you love giving birth, do you have any concerns for their safety? Think about what you have been told about birth: has it been negative or positive? What have you seen on TV or on the news?

We live in a culture where childbirth is seen as painful, difficult, and possibly even dangerous. Pregnancy and birth have always been a great passion of mine and I love to support women through this magical time with Chiropractic care. After a few years of doing this, I thought I should do the ultimate market research in this area, by experiencing it myself! This is when I discovered that being pregnant was also 'putting my money where my mouth is' in terms of testing how much I trusted my body. Even with all that I knew, I found being pregnant challenging because I had to work hard to filter out all the negative stories and comments about childbirth, so I could stay confident in my body.

The ideal place for any women to give birth is where she feels safest. For me, that is at home and so I planned a home birth for my first child. When people called me 'brave' for being at home, they didn't say it in a reassuring way. It was usually followed by the question, "What if something goes wrong?" My response was always *if,* not *when,* it does, then I'll head to hospital, thanks for the reassurance!

While complications do happen in childbirth, that doesn't mean we can't trust that the body (which is clever enough to create the baby) knows how to birth it. By helping a pregnant woman to trust her body, she is much more likely to feel calm, loved and safe during labour. This is what she needs to be flooded with the hormone oxytocin, which is essential for a smooth labour. Fear, anxiety and distrust in her own body and ability to give birth will create the opposite, unwanted effect.

Happily, we welcomed Beatrix at home on a Sunday morning after a smooth 4-hour labour. I believe my experience was so positive because I felt able to trust my body when the time came. That said, having that trust does not guarantee a specific outcome. But it does vastly change the experience. One client shared with me how, when she recognised her body was struggling during labour, she was able to be part of the decision-making process that led to her C-section. She did this by listening to her body, trusting its signal that she wasn't coping on her own, listening to that message and staying calm. Because she knew that she had followed her body, she thought it was a very good birth, despite it not going as she had planned. To me, this is a wonderful example of nature working in partnership with medicine.

One way to develop trust in your body is to build 'connection'. This can mean different things to different people but think of it as being 'in tune' or 'in touch' with your body. Connection happens when you can check-in and get feedback from your body and notice its signals. If you don't know how to connect with your body, it's very difficult to trust it. I remember discussing my impending birth experience with my older sister and she said that for her, waiting for labour to start had been "like waiting for an assassin to jump out and get me at any moment." While I didn't share that feeling, I understood exactly what she meant. It was only through staying connected to my body in a variety of ways all though my pregnancy, that I was able to feel quietly excited about my own labour.

When life calls upon you to put trust in your body, it is both challenging and revealing. It is also an opportunity for you to change your relationship with your body, to give you greater control over the experience, if not the outcome. After all, the natural cleverness that knew how to build your body in the womb, knows how to repair it now. Trusting your body makes a world of difference to how life feels on a daily basis because it allows you to feel stronger, calmer and more resilient. These are the feelings that you want when you need to rise to a challenge.

> HEALTH KEY
>
> The natural cleverness that knew how to build your body in the womb, knows how to repair it

Pain is your alarm system

I'm not going to get too far into this book before I talk about pain. After all, that's what a Chiropractor does, right? Helps back pain? Let me come back to that one! However, as a colleague of mine says, "It's all about the brain, it's not about the pain." He says this because your brain is the only area of your body where it's possible to feel pain. Pain is a signal in your nervous system that something may be wrong, and your brain is the only place in your body that receives and interprets that signal.

Imagine that you arrive home from the shops and the smoke alarm is screeching. What's the first thing you do? Do you press 'cancel' on the alarm, let yourself in and go about your day? Or do you look for the fire?

You notice smoke in a downstairs window, so you call the fire brigade. The firemen rush into the house, returning much quicker than you expected, holding two little round, white boxes. "If you take the batteries out, these alarms won't bother you again", one fireman tells you, smiling broadly as though the problem is solved. You don't smile. Surely you ask, "Why haven't you found the source of the fire? I saw smoke!"

When it comes to a fire at your house, you don't want to stop the disturbing alarm signal nearly as much as you want to discover why it went off in the first place. You would never leave a small fire burning in your kitchen and get on with your day. Why then, has the opposite become true when it comes to our pain? The body sends a pain signal to the brain and very often, our first course of action is to silence it with a painkiller, or ignore it completely. Pain is the best alarm system your body has, to tell you there's a problem. It is alerting you to a fire in progress. When your first instinct is to hide or ignore it, it's like living with that small fire in your kitchen. It's manageable at first, but you risk burning your house down.

When you trust that your body is clever, you know that symptoms happen for a reason. Pain is a symptom, and it happens for a reason. The pain isn't the problem, the problem is the problem. When you find and address that problem, you are putting out the fire and not just silencing the alarm. If you do choose to ignore the alarm, it costs you much more than simply living in discomfort. Ignoring your body's signals can impact every part of your life.

I will never forget the man who came into my office with intense lower back pain which would shoot down into his leg. He was clearly in pain that day as he limped around the office telling me his story. "How long have you been this way?" I asked, expecting him to say a few days or possibly a couple of weeks.

"Three years", he told me proudly with a smile. I could not smile back.

When I asked how he had managed to live for 3 years with such significant back pain, he explained how he had learned to eat meals and work standing up, and at the cinema he simply stood in an aisle. He was genuinely proud of the fact he had battled through as he saw it, for all that time.

The mindset of 'keep calm and carry on' makes me cringe inside. As a Chiropractor, I can't help thinking of the house burning down while its occupant calmly ignores it. I also know that by carrying on until the body breaks down, recovery is going to take much longer. Much easier to replace a burnt-out toaster than replace the whole kitchen. The fire that started in this man's back was spreading throughout his life. As a result of not being able to sit, he couldn't exercise and so he gained a lot of weight. He couldn't play with his young daughter, enjoy football with his friends or go on long car journeys without being in agony. After a while, he stopped travelling and socialising. Rather than empowering him, his desire to 'carry on' had taken away a lot of the things he enjoyed in life.

Thankfully, he chose to begin Chiropractic care and I was able to witness the wonderful change when he reconnected with his body, extinguished the fire, and began to heal. He also built trust in his body, so that in a matter of months he was sitting again, then he was able to return to exercise, lose the weight he had gained, have fun with his family and enjoy his body being a much friendlier place to live.

HEALTH KEY

Pain is a symptom, it happens for a reason. The pain isn't the problem, the problem is the problem

Nature is intelligent too

"You can live as though nothing is a miracle, or that everything is a miracle. I choose the latter" Albert Einstein

---

Just like in your body, millions of things are happening in the world around you whether you are conscious of them, or not. There are rhythms in the moon and tide, weather patterns form and change and on a global scale, temperatures change, ice melts and oceans rise. This in turn affects everything from the ecosystems and animals around you, to the weather you enjoy. You live on a planet where each part is intricately related to the other, although you may not always see the connection because the system is so big and complex. It is easier to only think about the world as it affects you, but there is so much natural cleverness within nature which reflects how your body works. Scientists are becoming aware of more incredible discoveries all the time.

In his book *The Hidden Life of Trees*, Peter Wohlleben describes what he calls the 'wood-wide web' where all the trees in a forest 'talk' to each other through chemical, hormonal and slow-pulsing electrical signals. These are like the electrical nerve impulses which travel through you, carrying messages between your body and brain through your spine. This is called your 'nervous system'. Like a nervous system, the forest has mushrooms and fungi growing at the base of these trees which form underground networks to transmit messages to each other. They send information about each tree, such as water and nutrient levels, and even send distress signals about drought and disease, or insect attacks which allows their neighbours to prepare for the attack. Wohlleben describes this as the tree's alarm or pain system.

In his research, Wohlleben recorded how other trees in the forest responded to these messages. Not only did he discover that trees would change their behaviour in response to a distress signal, but they effectively work as a community, with the tallest trees sharing nutrients from the sun with plants living in their shade. The idea of connection in the natural world should not feel new to us, after all, as a human being you are dependent on trees to keep the air clean enough for you to breathe. Nonetheless it is easy to miss the magic in nature because it's hard to see until you are looking for it.

We are only starting to become aware of the vast extent of cleverness that exists within nature. It is important to say that cleverness it is not the same as conscious thoughts or emotions, like the voice in your head. After all, a squirrel can remember the placement of thousands of nuts, choosing to leave some in the ground and cleverly ensuring the growth of his future food to come. The squirrel hasn't said to itself, "I had better leave this one or else there won't be any trees in the future", but the fact that this happens, through the way he naturally stores and retrieves his nuts, is a sign of natural cleverness.

Natural cleverness is a connection or a relationship with the world around you. You have probably experienced it when you go walking in nature and begin to feel calm, or that delightful feeling of being small and insignificant when surrounded by giant mountains. You experience it when you walk into a room and sense there has just been an argument, although everyone is behaving as though all is fine. Intuition and instinct are both forms of this cleverness: difficult to describe or control, but unquestionably real.

The cleverness in nature connects all of us as individuals, communities and as beings who share a planet. The more

I see this phenomenon in action, the more I feel it deserves our respect and protection. After all, scientists have found that on a molecular level, there is no definite boundary between the outer layer of your skin and the so-called outside world. We are a part of nature and nature is a part of us. Using this to your advantage can be a gamechanger when it comes to your health.

HEALTH KEY

The cleverness in nature connects all of us as individuals, communities and as beings who share a planet

A computer system – in your body!

"An acorn does not have to say I will become an oak tree, natural intelligence intends that every living thing become the highest form of itself and designs us accordingly" Mary-Ann Williamson

If I ask someone what a Chiropractor does, they will nearly always say it's someone who "treats back pain". This is understandable when your everyday view of health is in terms of solving problems however, this limiting description misses a much bigger picture. Yes, Chiropractors do work on your spine, but not because I am worried about your back pain. You might not even have any back pain, but you would still benefit from having your spine checked.

Your hard, bony yet flexible spine is a great example of natural cleverness, as it is perfectly designed to protect the most valuable part of your body – your spinal cord. Your spinal cord is a vast network of nerves which carries every piece of information from your body and the outside world, up into your brain and then takes the responsive messages from your brain back down into your body. Your central nervous system is like a master computer system controlling everything that happens inside you.

The entire list of 'things my body does without me even having to think about it', is only even possible because of this system. This constant feedback loop of information happens without you needing to think about it. If you think of your spinal cord as the trunk of a tree, large thick branches of spinal nerves exit the trunk in pairs down your spinal cord. These then branch off to reach every part of your body. Your spine protects the core trunk of wiring that makes up your internal computer system, but it also provides the door into influencing the system.

By working on the spine using gentle, specific impulses that we call 'adjustments', the signals can be changed as they pass to and from the brain. *This* is why Chiropractors focus on your spine! We look to restore the natural cleverness in your body, by making sure there are no issues with the flow of information connecting your body with your brain. Chiropractic isn't about taking away a problem (assuming you even have one) but maximising your body's ability to work at it's best.

Dr. Heidi Havvik is a Chiropractor in Australia, producing amazing research which shows how adjustments to your spine ultimately create changes to how your brain interprets and responds to signals. This is often called re-wiring. She has done a lot of work in people who are stuck in cycles of long term pain, where the brain can act as though it is still receiving a distressed pain signal, even when it is no longer being sent out by the body. This is why it is so important to look at how your nervous system is working as a whole, rather than focusing on a specific symptom.

In everyday terms, your brain is also wired to have thousands of learned patterns or habits, that we may want to change. Just waking up in the morning, getting out of bed, dressing, having your breakfast and brushing your teeth requires thousands of patterns your brain and body has learned over the years. Sitting and posture is a great example of this: how you sit when you are at work, school or in the car quickly becomes a habit that you don't give much thought to. That is until your shoulders or neck begin to ache. This can happen much earlier in life than you may expect, with a growing body of evidence showing musculoskeletal pain is becoming much more common in our school-age children. Our unconscious patterns in our physical movements and our mental thoughts, are constantly adding to the load on our nervous systems. When we change our brain's awareness of what is happening in the body on a daily basis, old patterns can start to be re-programmed.

So how can working on your spine affect different areas of your body? The answer lies in the huge number of branches coming off the tree trunk, aka your spinal cord. More than 7 trillion nerves reach out to every part of your body and track back to just 31 pairs of spinal nerves, which combine to make the spinal cord. For example, if you are having a heart attack, you experience pain down the left arm, chest and jaw. This is because the same nerve that keeps your heart beating also controls the muscles of your upper arm and skin in this area. In some way, every part of your body is connected to every other part.

Because the ability of your body to keep you moving, breathing, digesting, essentially *living*, all comes through this central system, I think it's very important that you understand how to keep your system running bug-free. There are two wonderful things about having a healthy central nervous system (I'll explain what I mean by *healthy* very soon). First is that the natural cleverness of your body means that when your system is in a good state, good things happen. Digestion works well, you sleep better, you have more energy and your body heals. Your body is designed to be in a regenerating state and is pre-programmed to make this happen. The second wonderful thing is that you then have more trust in your body, you feel able to accomplish new things and your body feels like a friendlier place to live.

The natural cleverness of your body knows how to keep you in a happy, healthy thriving state. When something interferes with this natural state of renewal, unwanted symptoms (like pain) begin to arise as a warning to your brain. Because of this, in Chiropractic we say health comes from top, down, inside, out (brain to body, inside to outside). This also explains why focussing on individual problems or symptoms can be unhelpful. More often than not, when the whole is well, the parts become well because the system is designed to make it happen.

HEALTH KEY

More often than not, when the whole is well, the parts become well because the system is designed to make it happen

Balancing your nervous system

"Health is a matter of choice, not a mystery of chance" Aristotle

---

Your nervous system influences every part of your body, so it ultimately affects every part of your life. It affects whether today is a good day, a bad day or a great day. Happily, your default setting is to thrive and repair, but how often do you really feel like your best self? As though you have so much energy you can achieve anything? Or do you feel a little tired, run down, sad or world weary? Unfortunately, it's not that easy to keep your nervous system balanced because for most of us, life isn't all that simple.

The reason it's so important to keep your nervous system in a state of balance is that your nervous system is ultimately responsible for your health. There are 3 key elements to health that I will address throughout this book:

Physical – The physical elements of your body including all the muscles, tendons, nerves, organs, brain and blood vessels. Structure is very important to allow your body to function as it was designed to, and protect against disease.

Emotional – How you think and feel has a direct impact on your body. It affects both how well the body functions and your motivation to maintain healthy habits. Your spiritual wellbeing (not necessarily religious) is also an important factor in emotional health.

Chemical – What you put into your body by way of food, drink, drugs and alcohol dictates how well your body can carry out its daily functions. It is constantly extracting nutrients, excreting waste and protecting us from disease. In a world full of hidden chemicals and toxins, your body is working hard to maintain a healthy chemical state.

When it comes to your nervous system, being *balanced* means that the amount of stress-relieving behaviours in your life actually balance or exceed the negative impact of the stressors. When you have more health than stress, your natural programming is to restore and grow. When there are more stressors than stress relievers, your system moves into a chemical state of stress where you can only survive, but not thrive. If the system is overwhelmed, it goes into a state you may know as 'fight or flight'. When you get stuck in this fighting or running state, in terms of your body chemistry, repair jobs in the body stop completely and your body begins to struggle and break down.

To be clear: a *stressor* is something which causes stress to your system like an unhealthy diet, slumped posture, a stressful job, demanding family or children, or simply the feeling of having too much on your plate and not enough time to do it all in. All of these things push your nervous system into *stress* which is a physiological response that happens to your body on a chemical level. In their book *Burnout,* the Nagoski sisters explain that even though you can take away the stress-causing behaviour (the stressor), your body or nervous system can still get stuck in that chemical state of stress which is damaging to your body. To get out of stress, your body needs a signal to tell it that it is safe.

Imagine you eat a fresh, organic diet, enjoy your job and have plenty of time for things that renew you: hobbies, exercise and time with friends or family. You're having a good time because you have more habits which support your nervous system than challenge it. Then you get a new job, have less time for your hobbies and exercises and experience a little more stress. You are just about balanced, able to still enjoy life but have lost that extra spark of energy you once enjoyed. As time passes, you realise the new job is much more demanding than you first thought, you become unhappy at work and find yourself collapsing on the sofa most nights with a quick dinner and glass of wine. You notice a few digestive upsets and your sleep isn't what it was.

Now your nervous system is beginning to show the tell-tale signs of having more negative stressors than positive lifestyle habits. If you carry on in this unbalanced state for months or even years, your nervous system can reach overwhelm. You get sick, blow a disc in your back, feel tired and achy, crave sugary foods, struggle to sleep through the night and never have regular bowel movements. Every one of your body systems is now in struggle. The same thing can happen if life suddenly becomes much more stressful for any reason, even for a short period of time. Your body acts like a transmission station for any stress that is going on in your life, so minimising stress and maximising health is the best way to feel comfortable in your body.

Understanding how this balancing act is playing out in your life gives you the opportunity to create your own health and happiness because you can make choices based on how it will affect the balance of your nervous system. It's also important to realise that the choices you have made in the past will always have an influence on your future. Like a car that has 100,000 miles on the clock and suddenly breaks down. It wasn't the steady drive you just took that caused it to breakdown, it was the years of tearing around corners at full speed, before you learnt to drive sensibly. For example, many of the people who have a heart attack in their fifties are experiencing the long-term consequences of how much they have eaten and exercised over their lifetime, not the last few years. How well your nervous system works for you today is affected by everything that has happened in your past.

HEALTH KEY

Your body acts like a transmission station for any stress in your life, so minimising stress and maximising health is the best way to feel comfortable in your body

What stresses YOUR body?

"That birds of worry and care fly over your head, this you cannot change. But

that they build nests in your hair, this you can prevent" Chinese proverb

---

It's easy to think of stress being 'bad' for you, however that's not always the case. Sometimes, you need a little stress to get things done and often good things like moving to a new house or starting a new job are stressful because they are new or effortful. The stressors in life are in themselves neither good nor bad. It's how well you are able to balance and control your stressors that matters.

The year 2014 was a big one for me: I moved to a new house, got married and bought my first Chiropractic office and left my old one... all within two weeks! I also squeezed a short honeymoon in there somewhere too. These were all exciting developments in my life, but it was a lot all at once. In the weeks leading up to this, I woke up one morning, went to stand up and passed out instead. My brain had pressed the 'off' switch and I collapsed to the floor. It happened a couple of times during that period. This was a clear sign that my nervous system had been overwhelmed by stress, even though everything I was doing was a positive step forward in my life, there were just too many at once.

Stressors are the internal and external factors in your life which put more demand on your nervous system. Some stressors you control, others you can't. For example, you can't always control being involved in a car accident, or getting bullied at work, loosing someone you love or your parents having divorced when you were a child. However, these all put more pressure on your nervous system because they can lead to a chemical state of stress in your body. When your body is in its stressed state, it is breaking down more than it is rebuilding, which is very damaging to your health (more on that later).

Stressors can be separated out into three main categories:

Physical stressors – Car accidents, falls, birth trauma (for mother or child), sports injuries, drunken mishaps, sitting at computers, binging on box sets, reading for hours in poor posture, driving or using a mobile phone. Physical stressors can cause damage to your spine and body (and therefore your nervous system too) either very suddenly or very slowly. Research has shown that spending lots of time hunched forward, as we all do, reduces the curve in your neck over the years. This reduction in neck curve reduces the pulmonary oxygen in your body by up to one third. You can experience the effect of this by sticking your neck forward right now and trying to take a deep breath, it's much harder. If your oxygen levels are reduced slightly for many years, the heart has to work harder, which puts you at more risk of heart problems. Your mother was right: good posture is very important!

Chemical stressors – Additives or chemicals in food, medications, alcohol, cigarettes, household cleaners, make-up, washing detergent, chemicals in your water supply and toxins in your environment. This also includes getting sick through virus or bacteria. Chemical stressors are all the things you put into your body that creates an extra load on your organs. If you happen to be intolerant to dairy for example, but continue to eat it, then a part of your body will constantly be stressed as you react to the dairy proteins. Like physical stressors, chemical stress is quiet and subtle, building up over many years.

Emotional and mental stressors – Being unhappy at work or school, going through a divorce, death, separation, being too busy, feeling out of your depth, struggling to fit in, feeling angry, frustrated or unheard. You don't have to think of yourself as unhappy to be under emotional stress. In fact, if you are an optimistic person, you will focus on a time in the future when the stress has passed or find a positive lesson from going through that stress and by looking for the silver lining, you are likely to think you are handling the stress well. A pessimistic person expects to feel dissatisfied at times and again, won't necessarily feel unhappy. Emotional and mental stress is almost impossible to avoid in our busy modern lifestyles.

Every one of these stressors has a direct physical impact on your body and your nervous system. Your organs work harder to filter out impurities, your immune system can become over-reactive, your joints wear out more quickly, you lose mobility and flexibility, you develop pain or digestive problems. I could go on and on. In truth, you are never experiencing only one stressor at a time, but multiple stressors over multiple years. Is it easier to see why your body might not be working at it's very best?

Stressors can add up suddenly, until you become mentally overwhelmed and physically exhausted, like I did. When this happens, it's difficult to ignore so you usually do something about it. The subtle stressors which build up over many years are much more dangerous to your health and happiness in my opinion, because you often don't notice them until it's too late. Your nervous system doesn't go from conducting every action in your body perfectly, to suddenly breaking down (unless something catastrophic happens). In reality, over many years, small changes or compensations start to appear that you accept as a normal part of life. You carry on until you reach a point where enough function has been lost that you think of asking for help. Just like putting off your diet until your jeans feel super tight, the subtle signals that your nervous system has too many stressors are there, but easy to ignore.

While you can't remove all the stressors in your life, you can become more consciously aware of them. By taking notice, you are making the first step towards creating positive change for yourself and taking back control of your health and future happiness.

HEALTH KEY

The stressors in your life are themselves neither good nor bad. It's how well you are able to balance and control your stressors that matters for your health

Why fight or flight matters

"When all you know is fight or flight, red flags and butterflies all feel the same" Cindy Cherie

You are probably already aware of your body's fight or flight response, which happens automatically any time you feel threatened. Your brain quickly assesses whether your best chance of survival is to approach and fight, or run and flee. Your brain releases a cascade of chemicals into your body, affecting every part of it. Fight or flight is a chemical state of stress in your body and it is a response of your nervous system. It looks like this:

- Increasing muscle tension ready to fight or flee
- Increasing your heart rate so more oxygen is available
- Switching off the reasoning part of your brain so you can react quickly
- Releasing hormones like adrenaline so you feel wide awake and don't do anything unsafe, like falling asleep
- Stopping digestion, while releasing the lower digestive tract
- Stopping other non-essential activities such as healing or fighting bugs with your immune system (no time for that right now, thank you)!

The fight or flight response helps to keep you safe and alive. However, your body is wired to be in a stress or survival state based on how safe you *feel*, not how safe you actually *are*. This means that something that isn't life threatening can still cause you to have a survival response. For example, having an argument with a friend, someone cutting you up on the motorway and giving you a scare, or even feeling like you are being 'chased' by a never-ending list of tasks and responsibilities. Humans are emotional beings who think, not thinking beings who sometimes feel emotions. This means that while you rationally *know* that your life isn't in danger, you *feel* under pressure, which can easily kick off the fight or flight response in your body.

In everyday life, signs that your body is stuck in this chemical state of stress can look like this:

- Struggling to concentrate, make decisions or absorb vast amounts of new information
- Finding yourself snapping at others, or over-reacting to situations
- Difficultly dropping off, staying asleep or waking in the morning not feeling rested
- Being aware of holding tension in your shoulders, neck and jaw, or clenching your teeth
- Experiencing digestive upsets like bloating, cramping, diarrhoea, heart burn or constipation, even just around one particular food group
- Always catching the office cold or feeling run down
- Struggling to find the energy or motivation to get things done
- Wondering why something hasn't healed or got better when you expected it to
- Finding yourself hunched forward or curled in on yourself

The signs that your body is in stress can be very subtle and you can often learn to live with them, accepting your less than ideal health. Whenever your body is in this state of chemical stress, you are not repairing, healing or thriving. Instead, your body is limited to its basic functions which makes life feel more like a struggle. Think of it like using the last of your mobile phone charge to make an important phone call, you can do this most basic function, however there is not enough extra power for you to open an app or browse the web.

Finding yourself in fight or flight is easy to do, because of all the stressors you encounter on a daily basis. Even when the stressors go, your brain and body can remain in a state of chemical stress until you receive the message that you are safe. The more often you experience being in fight or flight, or if you live in that state for a long time, the process becomes quicker and easier to activate in your body. Even remembering or imagining a stressful experience can create the physical response in your body. The threat doesn't have to be truly threatening or even exist, for your body to enter a state of chemical stress. However, the more often it happens, the easier it is for even minor stressors to cause major impact on how your nervous system is working.

Simply put, it easier than ever to live in physiological stress and for modern culture to keep us there.

HEALTH KEY

Whenever your body is in a state of chemical stress, you are not repairing, healing or thriving

Are you aware of the stress?

"In reality, what you experience is a mirror image of your expectations"
Deepak Chopra

I am the proud owner of a gorgeous pug called Jelly. He is very noisy as his flat face means he cannot breathe without snorting or grunting and his snoring is so loud you can hear it from two floors up. Does it bother me? I don't even notice it! My brain is so used to hearing his deep rumbling snores, they no longer register. The only time I notice them is when someone new comes to my Chiropractic studio and asks, "What on earth is that noise?" and I look around in confusion, having forgotten he's even in there.

The natural cleverness in your body means that your brain is designed to filter out everything you see, hear, smell and feel that you don't need to be aware of in that moment. If it didn't do this, how would you ever get anything done? Traffic driving past your window, the smell of your shower gel, the feel of clothes touching your skin and hundreds of other small details would be so distracting if you were aware of them all time. The same thing happens when it comes to many of the stressors in your environment. Being constantly busy: daily negotiations with children and family, the dull ache in your back when you sit, the tension in your shoulders that you press absentmindedly, they all become part of the 'normal' fabric of your life. Once you have experienced something for a while your brain simply lets it drift off into the background, assuming it's not important.

When you live with stressors without noticing them, they begin to impact your nervous system. A classic example is the schoolteacher who finds themselves getting sick every time school holidays come around. Her body was already in stress and breaking down, but her brain didn't have the available bandwidth to process it. Instead, she pushed on until during those first precious days off her brain is finally able to register the stress she has been under and she begins to feel terrible. Like a car engine running on petrol fumes, once the engine is finally switched off, it won't turn back on without being refilled. Many professional jobs are like this: with expectations and deadlines to meet, combined with personal commitments to family and friends, it's very difficult to stay un-stressed in the modern world. I would go as far as to say it's nearly impossible to do it without conscious effort.

Researchers believe that your body is designed to live in a state of relaxation approximately 80 percent of the time. You were designed to be in fight or flight (stress) less than

20 percent of your life. However, if you switched those numbers, it would probably represent the reality of how we live today. That glorious feeling which travels all the way down your body when you first realise you are on holiday, and you sigh as a big wave of contentment travels through your body, that is the feeling of ease in your central nervous system. How often do you experience this feeling in your daily life?

Because you do encounter stressors on a regular basis and your brain is designed to filter them out, or cope so that you can still get things done, how can you tell if your body is in stress? A lifestyle assessment is a good place to start. Taking a broader view of every aspect of your life including the physical, chemical and emotional factors will start to give you an indication. If you recognise some of the signs of fight or flight listed above, then your nervous system is likely to be experiencing some chemical stress. Talking to a professional who can take an overview of your health and help you see where you can make changes is a great place to start making a change.

HEALTH KEY

Once you have experienced something for a while, your brain simply lets it drift into the background, assuming it's not important

How to manage stress

The analogy of a kitchen sink is a great one for understanding how stressors show up in your life and the steps you can take to reduce them.

Imagine you have a brand new kitchen. It's absolutely beautiful and cost every penny of your savings because you went all out. You hand-picked every part: the sink, the taps the worktops, the tiles and the floor. Naturally, you want to start cooking right away because a kitchen like yours was designed to be enjoyed. You eat a wonderful meal and decide to wash the wine glasses by hand (they are too nice for your fancy new dishwasher). However, when you go to turn on the taps, the water gushes out and won't stop. You can't control it! Your sink is swiftly filling up with water and about to spill onto your beautiful new floor and damage it permanently. How can you stop it from happening?

The water gushing out from the taps represents the stress pouring into your life, which can happen quickly or slowly. The sink represents the extra capacity your nervous system has to deal with those stressors. If you don't have much capacity, your sink will be small and fill more quickly than someone who has a greater tolerance for stress. That's why comparing what you can cope with, compared to other people, is not helpful. The water (or stress) spilling over the side may be a splash you can quickly mop up, or it could consistently drip onto your new floor, slowly rotting it over time.

In this scenario, there are two main ways you can rescue your floor: pull the plug out of the sink and turn the taps down. So what does this look like in real life?

When you effectively 'pull the plug' on your stress, this means making space for all the things that allow you to let go of stress. The key is that when you notice the stress flowing in more rapidly than you would like, you make whatever it is that releases stress for you, your top priority.

Whatever it is that helps release your stress is unique to you. Think of something you do where you lose track of all time, that's a good sign that you are releasing stress. It can be time spent with friends, meditation, going for a walk, relaxing in a bath, taking the time to cook a nourishing meal from scratch or doing a workout. Generally, these are the things we let slide when we have too much on. Things that make you laugh, fill our imagination or help you connect with other people are great stress relievers, like playing in a band or visiting the cinema with friends. Other things you can do for your body and mind which will reduce the feelings of stress and create more ease in the body include doing some form of physical exercise (doesn't have to be strenuous), resting and breathing deeply.

You can also 'turn the taps down' as much as possible by simplifying what's happening to you at that time. Learning to say "no" is often helpful for this. The important thing to realise about stress relievers is that they are rarely an instant fix but if you do them consistently, you will get a much better result.

In the overflowing sink scenario, there is a third possible way to rescue your floor – get a bigger sink. It is possible for you to increase your natural capacity for stress, however it takes time and commitment. Creating a life with built-in stress releasers is the best way for you to stay happy and healthy into the future, which is why the whole of the final chapter of this book is full of practical ways you can do this for yourself.

You can begin by noticing how full your 'sink' is and try to reduce the water levels long before you are reaching your limit. There will always be times when stress threatens to overwhelm you, but now you can be proactive and make your stress releasers a priority. After all, you can support everyone around you much better when you already have that extra capacity for them in your life.

HEALTH KEY

You can't pour from an empty cup, take care of yourself first

The power of placebo

When I was 13, I started experiencing awful migraines that would keep me in bed and out of school for days. My doctor prescribed some bright pink and yellow tablets but they didn't usually do anything for me and the migraine would come anyway. Even as a child, it didn't make sense to me that my only options were to live with the headaches or take a pill. My dad agreed so he took me to see his friend Liz. She was a medically trained doctor, but also a homeopath and cranio-sacral therapist. I went to see her regularly for about 6 months and she would spend a lot of time asking me about my life and give me cranial therapy. At the end of each session, Liz would hand me a little brown envelope with tiny white pills that I was to let dissolve under my tongue over the coming days.

At 13, I didn't understand anything about what she was doing with her questions, gentle hands and little pills. Over time however, my migraines became less frequent until eventually they stopped. I was really happy to get back to my normal teenage life and not have to go back on medication. Ever since then, I have told people that homeopathy helped stop my migraines. But most people respond by saying 'homeopathy is only placebo' – I don't think I've turned many people onto the idea of trying it for themselves. But what is placebo? And is it such a bad thing?

Placebo is your brain's ability to create change in your body, simply by believing that change should happen. Scientists did a study where one group of people learned to play the piano while a second group imagined practicing the piano in their heads. The third group as a control group, did nothing. In both the first and second groups, there was a measurable increase in the finger strength of participants. Even the group who only imagined their fingers moving over the keys, had created a noticeable change in the strength of their fingers. As you would expect, the finger strength of the people in the control group had not changed. This experiment shows how simply *thinking* something in your brain can create a measurable physical response in your body. This is the power of placebo.

Another good way to experience placebo is to imagine you are sucking on a lemon as you read this. Notice how your mouth fills with saliva? Just expecting to taste that sour lemon causes the saliva in your mouth to increase, even though the fruit is not physically there. Body builders use this to their advantage by focussing their mind on the muscle they are using as they lift their weights. Bringing the brain on board allows the muscle to build strength more quickly. All of these are examples of placebo and confirmation of the incredible power your brain has over your body.

This idea that placebo means 'not useful or valid', is simply not true. The pharmaceutical industry knows this, which is why every new medication is tested against a placebo (fake) pill, rather than no pill at all. They know that a medicine is only considered effective, if the group of people taking the drug have better results than the group that simply believe they have taken the drug. Just like in the piano experiment, often both groups experience some changes.

The opposite of placebo is not, as you might assume, no change at all. The opposite of placebo is *nocebo*. Nocebo is the term which describes what happens in your body when your brain expects something negative to happen to you. For example, reading all the side-effects of a medication and slowly finding yourself developing them. As I explained before, just *imagining* a stressful situation such as imagining how a difficult conversation may turn into an argument, will create a physical stress response in your body. It doesn't matter the event isn't actually happening to you, only that your brain believes it. Have you ever been nervous about giving a presentation and felt your muscles tighten and hunger levels reduce? Your brain is creating a protective response in your body that it expects you to need.

The placebo effect comes into all parts of our lives, whether we are aware of it or not. The placebo effect is very real, often positive and you can use it to your advantage. While the automatic, unconscious part of your brain is constantly controlling your body through your nervous system, the conscious part of your brain also affects how your body works. If I am struggling to lift a weight in the gym, I have found that asking a friend to support me suddenly makes the weight feel lighter. They are not taking any weight for me (in fact this trick works even if they lay only a fingertip under the heavy bar) but my belief that my body is strong enough to lift it with support, makes it happen.

Your brain and your body are intricately linked on many levels. What would it mean for you to start trusting that your body is clever, strong and capable of healing? How would that impact your enjoyment of life?

HEALTH KEY

The placebo effect is scientific proof that we have the ability to heal ourselves. That our thoughts are powerful enough to bring things into existence

Your three brains. Yes, three.

"The best decisions aren't made with your mind, but with your instinct"
Lionel Messi

Since your expectations create your reality, what you believe in your mind, tends to become your reality. This is the confusing logic of the brain in your head: the master processor which perceives and interprets the world around you. By this point, you may have started to question whether the world as you experience it is real, or a trick of your mind. So where do you go when you don't know what to trust? Hopefully, to your instincts.

When an explorer goes into a new forest, they mark a tree. This is their 'touch tree' that they can always return to. No matter which path they take, or how far down a track they travel, so long as they can find their way back to their marked tree, the explorer cannot get lost. On returning to their touch tree, they know exactly where they are and can easily decide which way to go next. You have your own version of a touch tree within yourself, a way of checking-in with feelings and emotions in a place much deeper than your brain. If you've ever found yourself saying, "I'm getting too stuck in my own head" or "My brain thinks this but my gut or my heart knows differently", then you may be aware that there are different levels of instinct or knowing within your body.

Your instinct or spirit is the third element of your nervous system, along with your body and brain. I use the term *spirit* to mean the unique way that you see and relate to the world. Your spirit is what makes the elements of your brain and body work in a particular way compared to someone else. It is your own expression of natural cleverness. Your spirit is very closely linked with your ethics and values (more on this later) and if you are not living in a way that matches with your internal self, it will create that chemical stress state in your body. For example, regularly carrying out a task that causes you to feel unhappy, unsupported or frustrated isn't physically harmful, but it is harmful to your spirit and so it will negatively impact your health.

Perhaps one of the reasons that spiritual health can feel uncomfortable or unreal for people, is that there isn't an organ in your body where your spirit is known to live. Research in psychology shows that people refer to their head, heart or gut while making important decisions in different areas of their lives. Your 'gut brain' is thought to hold your immune system and is linked to feelings of self-preservation, fear, anxiety, mobility and action. As you now know, your gut is also linked to your fight or flight response. Scientists have found that re-seeding the gut with bacteria from a healthy person helps people to overcome depression. I think that's incredible!

Your 'heart brain' is usually where you turn regarding relationships and values. As you experience feelings and instincts in different parts of your body, researchers have created this concept of having 3 brains. Although not physically true, it reinforces the idea of your body working as a whole system, rather than several disconnected parts. Moving your attention into different parts of your body allows you to see that your thoughts are not who you are, only one small part of a much bigger picture.

Think of your thoughts, feelings and emotions as being like rain; you experience the wetness of the rain, but you are not the rain. You walk through it and come out of the other side. Author Marc Allen describes the concept of 'the watcher' – the calm, inner part of yourself which is able to distance itself from whatever strong emotion you are experiencing and observe it almost as though it is happening to another person. The watcher gives insight into what you really want and reassurance that you are doing the right thing. When you discover your ability to watch yourself reacting, you can step out of your brain space, into another space. This is checking in with gut instinct or with your spirit. It is an important part of being able to see all the elements of stress at play in your life and finding the next logical step in restoring your balance.

HEALTH KEY

Your instinct or spirit is the third element of your nervous system, along with your body and brain

Learn to trust and move forward

The planet you call home is richly interconnected. The cleverness in nature also exists within your body. It is designed to protect you and keep you alive. Your challenge is to trust in your own natural intelligence and try to respond to what it tells you. Everything you think, feel or do, both knowingly and unknowingly, impacts your nervous system and influences how you experience life.

Keeping trust in your body becomes difficult when you are used to living in a chemical state of stress, because this makes you feel unsafe on a basic physiological level. This is why it is easy to feel disconnected from your body, or as though you can't trust it. Modern culture has made it easy to lose track of what great health looks like for you, and to accept being 'less than' as normal. You begin to miss the signs that your nervous system is out of balance, until the symptoms become impossible to ignore.

If you can accept that your body is clever and strong, and that it is capable and designed to protect you, how does that change how you feel about your body? How does it change how you look at your own health?

Chapter 2: How We Think About Health

My turning point

"Nature needs no help, just no interference" *BJ Palmer*

Around 2 years after graduating from Chiropractic college, I was driving home from work one day when my mum called me. I answered on the car phone, "What are you doing?" she asked. "Driving home from work", I replied. "Well don't crash the car", she said, "but I have cancer." My mum was a fit, slim 56-year-old woman who ran regularly and did yoga. She never smoked or drank alcohol, even as a teenager. She was not someone who any doctor would expect to have stomach cancer, traditionally a 65-year-old smoking man's disease.

That one conversation with my mum turned my world upside down. As a health professional I felt I should have noticed the signs that something was wrong. Except there weren't many signs, other than some digestive upsets which her GP had assumed was an irritable bowel. As her daughter, I was bewildered that my mum, who seemed so fit, strong and healthy on the outside, could be so sick on the inside. It blew apart the idea that how someone *feels* is a reliable way of knowing how healthy they are.

At the time I was still in the 'Chiropractic really helps people with back pain to heal naturally and improve their life' way of thinking. Nothing wrong with that, except suddenly it seemed too simplistic. I could be missing something important, like I had with my mum. I wanted to care for my clients as a whole person, looking beyond their pain or problem, to help them lead the best life possible. I needed to find an accurate, more thorough way of measuring how healthy someone was. I also needed to let go of the idea that pain is a reliable guidepost of health. My mum didn't have pain until her cancer reached an advanced stage.

Over the next few years, I made it my mission to find better ways to measure health: looking at lifestyle, stress and happiness alongside pain and physical movement. I studied neurology and learned how to assess nervous system function and whether the information is flowing well between body and brain. I came to realise that although my mum always *looked* healthy, she had a history of depression, never slept well and constantly craved sugar. I learned how these are all indications that her body was in a state of chemical stress which as you now know, causes the body to break down, rather than rebuild. Mum never suspected she had cancer and missed more subtle signs that came before the pain. I believe she had probably become disconnected from her body over the years and wasn't used to hearing and interpreting its signals.

Just 10 weeks after that phone conversation, my mum had died from end stage stomach cancer. She never retired, never saw me open my practice or get married. She has never met my daughter Beatrix Moira who I named after her. I have experienced first-hand, how devastating it is to lose a loved one through ill health and I want to help you avoid the same, by showing you the importance of staying connected to your body. To be listening for the natural cleverness within you to tell your brain "something's not quite right here." Or, even if a diagnosis is the first you are aware of an illness, that you feel able to trust your body and work in partnership with it.

I feel unbelievably lucky that I was already a Chiropractor when my mum died. The way Chiropractors view the body: as clever, whole, connected and part of nature, has helped me to make sense of what happened and take something good from it. With every new client I meet, I hold my mum in mind. I make it my mission to help that person take a broader view of their life and how they want to enjoy it. I introduce them to the miracle that is their nervous system and how they can create more balance and ease in their life. I try to prevent them from becoming so focussed on solving the problem they have come in with, that they forget to look at the bigger picture.

HEALTH KEY

Avoid becoming so focussed on solving the problem you have, that you forget to look at the bigger picture of your life and health

The sick-care model of health

I have lost count of the number of times a new client has come to my office explaining, "My doctor told me to wait until I can't cope with it anymore and then to go back to him. But I'm hoping there's something that can be done about it now." Somehow the system designed to care for our *health* has become based on you being *sick* enough to need help.

The title 'doctor' actually comes from the Latin verb docēre meaning 'to teach'. You were meant to go to the doctor not so they could heal you, but so they could teach you how to become well. The saying goes, "Give a man a fish and he can eat for a day but teach him to fish, and you feed him for a lifetime." For me, the same is true for your health. You can take a pill for your problem and keep asking for more pills, or the doctor can teach you how to resolve or avoid the problem in the first place.

Of course, depending on what your problem is, your body may not be able to heal itself, or avoid another episode. Nature is amazing but it does have limits. I prefer to choose the natural option first and turn to medicine only when nature cannot take me the full way. Given that lifestyle related diseases cost the struggling NHS £11 billion in 2016, there is clearly a need for all of us to better understand how our lifestyle choices affect our health. Otherwise, we may not have a healthcare system to turn to in future. By inviting you to be involved in your own health journey, there is an opportunity to create a partnership that empowers both doctor and patient.

From early childhood we are taught that patients are unknowing and vulnerable, and doctors hold all the answers. Most of us were taken to the doctor if we became sick and promised, "the medicine will make you better". Even our nursery rhymes reinforce the idea: "Miss Polly had a dolly who was sick sick sick, so she called for the doctor to be quick quick quick." And what does the doctor do? "She wrote on her paper for a pill, pill, pill…" The idea of the doctor as healer is engrained so early on, we never think to question it. You feel comforted believing someone will come along and make everything better. However, this way of thinking also denies the central role you play in your own health and helps you forget the natural cleverness in your body. This imbalance of power means that when medicine doesn't have a solution to your problem, you are left feeling scared and abandoned and believing you have nowhere else you can turn. Trusting that your body is naturally designed to heal, despite all the odds, can be great comfort.

Our current healthcare system isn't empowering you. Instead, it gives us permission to make choices that we know are bad for our health, under the belief that there will be a pill to take care of the consequences. Then when the system becomes overwhelmed with sick people, it blames us for not making better choices. Our doctors and nurses are overstretched, stressed and become sick themselves. We have created a system where both doctor and patient suffer. By taking the time to read this book and look at different ideas around health, you have the ability to help the NHS, re-claim your self-worth and potentially save your own life.

HEALTH KEY

When you pursue your own health, you have a say in your future and re-claim your self-worth

What does it mean to be healthy?

The word 'healthy' means different things for different people. I like the definition from the World Health Organisation (WHO) who clarify two important points:

- Health is a state of complete physical, mental and social well-being and not merely the absence of disease or infirmity.
- The enjoyment of the highest attainable standard of health is one of the fundamental rights of every human being without distinction of race, religion, political belief, economic or social condition.

In other words, health is reflected in every aspect of your life: physically, mentally and emotionally. This is why I assess my client's ability to heal by addressing each of these areas. As you now know, for you to be healthy, the stressors in your life cannot exceed the capacity of your nervous system to deal with that stress. The way I view health isn't a unique quirk of being a Chiropractor, it's actually the definition the world has agreed on!

In its definition, the WHO highlights the fact that health isn't just about not being sick, there is more to it than that. The goal is to achieve the 'highest attainable standard of health' in other words *thriving*. Sickness is not the opposite of being healthy: sickness is simply a state better than dead. Like a ladder, there are many rungs between death (the bottom rung) and thriving (the top of the ladder). Each rung represents the balance of stressors and health in your nervous system and this book is designed to help you figure out which rung you are currently on, and how to climb up to the next one.

The other important thing about the WHO definition of health is that it reflects a fundamental truth: that health comes from inside of you. Your physical, mental and social wellbeing aren't controlled by any outside organisation or force. You decide what to take from doctors and health services, whether to see a Chiropractor, or use a personal trainer. Each choice helps create a change inside of you, bringing you closer to, or further away from thriving.

Knowing that you are responsible for your health is empowering, but also daunting. It's tempting to hope that someone will come along and get you back on track without you having to ask. Sadly though, there are competing forces in the political and business worlds that mean you need to be the one looking out for you. In the Covid-19 pandemic, the NHS ran adverts telling you to lose weight because heart disease and diabetes made you more likely to die of the virus. At the same time, the government offered you vouchers to eat at McDonald's, while keeping the gyms closed. There are a lot of mixed messages when it comes to health, so learning how to see through the fog and make decisions for yourself is important. The person who will always be in the best position to help you get healthier and live a better life, is you.

HEALTH KEY

Health comes from the inside you and radiates out, not from outside sources

Redefining health and healing

During my time as a nursing assistant, I was offered the opportunity to spend a day observing autopsies. As someone who has been fascinated by the human body since childhood, this made me nervous and excited in equal measure. It was a Thursday morning in late Autumn, and I can still remember in distinct detail the 3 autopsies I witnessed that day. A young boy who had been in a car crash and suffered a brain haemorrhage, an elderly lady with a stroke who had fallen down the stairs, and a middle-aged man with a body full of lymphoma. Something profound struck me that day: I realised that whatever happens when we die, the body is simply a shell for our spirit.

Imagine you buy a beautiful Rolex watch to pass down to future generations of your family. If it stops working, you can find a skilled craftsman to fix it. He can take it fully apart, replace every piece and re-assemble it. The ticking that signals a watch's life is easily restored with the right knowledge and tools. However, I could bring in all the best doctors, surgeons and scientists in the world, give them all the money in the world, and still that young boy who died in the car crash couldn't be brought back to life. When the natural cleverness in your body stops alongside your heartbeat, the intangible spark of life, your true essence, your spirit, cannot be restored. This is the perfect example of the whole being much greater than the sum of his parts.

The word 'healing' has the same root as the word 'wholeness' so it makes sense that to be 'healthy' we need to be 'whole'. I don't mean all in one piece, because hopefully you are! When every part of your body works to its best, your mind is calm and you are emotionally fulfilled, your potential to achieve things increases exponentially. This is wholeness in terms of your health, and it is what allows your body to heal. Healing is the ability for your cells to regenerate and renew in life and is what truly sets us apart from death. As the surgeon completed each autopsy, he carefully stapled the skin back in place, knowing that the body could no longer repair itself and fuse the skin back together naturally. Healing is the ability for your cells to regenerate and renew in life and is what truly sets us apart from death. Life, in its simplest form is renewal.

You have an 'X factor' that even the best scientists cannot fully explain. Rather than resisting or denying what science cannot understand, I prefer to honour and respect the magic of your unique natural cleverness. When information flows between your body and brain through your spine, without interference from stress, your body remains in a natural state of renewal. In other words, it is constantly keeping itself whole.

Maintaining this connection is how Chiropractors can help make sure each part of your body system can work at its best. Because of this, we don't see any particular symptom as more important than another. Every sign from the body has equal importance. From a holistic viewpoint, an irritated digestive system needs healing as much as a cut finger, or a trapped nerve. A feeling of low energy needs healing as much as a cold. The whole is always more important than one part.

If being healthy means that you need to be healing, then the idea of addressing just one area of your life at a time doesn't make sense. Instead of choosing yoga ***or*** running, mindfulness ***or*** good sleep, a salad ***or*** Chiropractic care, do as many of them as you can. When you practice yoga, run, relax, sleep, eat well ***and*** receive Chiropractic adjustments, you are really contributing to your whole: your whole health, your whole life experience, and your whole future.

HEALTH KEY

The whole is much greater than the sum of its parts

How do I know if I'm healthy?

Health is a state of wholeness and renewal so looking at just one tiny element of your life can't give an accurate picture of your overall health. Many factors in your health fluctuate even within the course of a day: mood, energy, body weight and pain levels. Using just one of these to make an accurate assessment of your health is like trying to guess the picture on a 1000-piece jigsaw from just one piece.

Other important indicators of your health include:

- energy levels
- body and brain connection
- happiness and life satisfaction
- emotional stress
- consistency and quality of sleep
- digestion
- posture
- range of motion
- diet and nutrition

- habits and hobbies
- balance and co-ordination
- how often you become sick and how quickly you recover
- changes in physical structure
- hormone levels

Health is so complex because it is part of this 'wholeness' of being, with thousands of physical, mental and chemical components that are expressed and experienced in your own unique way. The more of these components that are measured, the clearer the picture becomes. Remember, some signs of good health feel counterintuitive. Developing diarrhoea, stomach cramps and vomiting is a healthy response to food poisoning. It is a very efficient way for your body to get rid of the bacteria in your gut and restore a healthy state. If you looked at these symptoms in isolation, it would be easy to reach the wrong conclusion.

Knowing you are healthy means taking a broad view of your life and seeing whether you are in a state of renewal. That means, are these areas improving, being maintained or are they getting worse? The answer will change as you move through different phases in your life. Becoming aware of your body's signals and your life stressors allows you to re-balance quickly and easily.

HEALTH KEY

If you do not make time for your wellness, you may be forced to make time for your illness

Are you heading for a cruise ship or care home?

"The whole of Western medicine is built on getting rid of pain, which is not the same as healing." Gabor Mate

---

Imagine yourself aged 72. You have enjoyed a busy and successful life and retired early enough to have several decades to enjoy between finishing work and dying. Think about how you've changed over the years, and ask yourself:

- What does my face look like now?
- How has my body changed?
- What do you I like to do with my time?
- Where am I going? Am I travelling?
- Where do I live? Independently? In a care home?

- Can I still jump on a cruise ship or aeroplane ready to explore the world?

Come back into your body now, in this time. With the lifestyle choices you are making today, which one are you heading towards: the care home or the cruise ship? The choices you make today create the foundation for your future, alongside all the choices you have made in the past. This is especially true of the physical, chemical and emotional factors that control whether your nervous system is in a state of stress.

My dream at 72 when I picture it, is myself and my husband still slim and fit enough to be hiking up some beautiful mountains. To spend our time walking great trails around the world, admiring the view. We are easily able to recover from the travel, changing time zones and different beds. We are still able to enjoy our freedom.

The way I think about my future self has changed quite significantly after recently reading reports on a growing area of science in 'epigenetics'. Epigenetics are little bits of code on your genes that your body switches on and off in response to your environment. As Ruby Wax explains in her book *No-Brainer,* if your genes were a cake recipe which read: "Mix the butter and sugar together", the epigenetics part would be a handwritten note on the side reading: "Use the butter at room temperature". Scientists of epigenetics are exploring how your perceptions and expectations can also influence your biology and cause certain genes to switch on and off. This has the potential to affect the outcome of your entire life!

So, in the past I used to say, "I like to live every day to the full because I might die at 56 like my mum did." While I meant it in a positive way, intending to make the most of every moment, this thought process also reinforced my belief that I will die young of cancer. This is not an expectation I want to hold true for myself consciously or not. Realising this, I worked hard to get a clear image of myself well into my 70s and 80s, strong, fit and exploring the world. How you imagine your future, helps to create it because you are naturally led to making decisions that are likely to produce the results you expect. Of course, it's not enough to simply imagine yourself healthy and thriving in later life and expect it to just happen. Years of maintaining a healthy, balanced nervous system is important. But, looking *forward* to good health can be a valuable tool to help you take positive action.

Neuroscience shows that whenever you set a goal, your sub-conscious mind sets about looking for ways to make that goal a reality. For example, if you decide to join a gym, you will start noticing gyms and health classes being advertised on your daily commute that you never saw there before. Because you now want that information, the sub-conscious part of your brain stops filtering it away from your conscious awareness. In contrast, if you choose to focus on what you *don't* want: to be sick, to die young, to feel stressed all the time, your brain can't help you in the same way. How can it help you look for something you don't want to find?

Concentrating on building your health is much more powerful than focussing on what's wrong or intending to avoid sickness. When you have a clear picture of your future self, enjoying life in every way you can, you instinctively find the next step to getting there. Just as the money you save over many years builds into a retirement fund you can enjoy, your health needs its own retirement fund of many small actions. By beginning with the end in mind you can consciously choose cruise ships over care homes and not leave it to chance.

HEALTH KEY

With the lifestyle choices you are making today, which one are you heading towards: the care home or the cruise ship?

Can you 'fix' a Human Being?

Think about the different ways you could describe your health – terrible, fair, OK, quite good, excellent, amazing etc. Each term is a rung on a ladder all the way from dead to the best you can possibly be, right at the top. Where is your health on the ladder right now? Anywhere from the middle upwards and you might not have any significant health issues that you are aware of, however you probably have several areas such as sleep, mood or hormone regulation that you would like to improve. You don't need to have a problem to benefit from becoming healthier.

It is also never too late to start making positive changes even if you feel 'broken' and have done for a long time. You have simply moved further down the ladder and need to climb a few steps up. Sometimes you need the help of a professional to get climbing again. The truth is that even when you are thriving at the top of the ladder, there is no guarantee that you won't experience any health problems. No matter your situation, your nervous system will always be balancing stress and have the potential to become overwhelmed. The further up the ladder of health you climb, the more ready you are to meet the challenge head on.

Imagine driving your car down the motorway every day and a warning light comes on. The car still seems to be going, there are no alarming noises, so you continue in the hope that the light switches off as mysteriously as it came on. You hope that this first warning signal turns out to be nothing but it's difficult to feel relaxed every time you drive with it still on. In the same way, it's much more difficult to live life in ease when you are ignoring signals from your body.

If the warning turns into *something* you tend to wish you'd paid attention earlier. The fateful day arrives when the grinding, clunking noise you've been expecting kicks in and you find your car in limp mode. The in-built computer has decided to stop you from doing irreparable damage to the engine. This is your car's version of developing pain – stop the system from becoming so damaged it can never recover.

So, you take your car to a mechanic who can fix it. But this experience has cost you – time, money, inconvenience. You don't want to make it a regular thing. In an ideal world, you would like to make sure your car never develops a fault again. The mechanic explains "The only way I can fix your car so that it *never* breaks again, is to not let you drive it at all." Your mechanic knows there is no way to fix any dynamic system that means it won't break again.

Accidents and illness happen to healthy people, so the idea of a 'fix' is misleading. Just as you keep your car clean, serviced and topped up with fuel so it runs at its best for many years, your body also needs consistent care and attention. By keeping your car serviced you are confident the brakes will work during an emergency stop. In the same way, taking care of your health can give you confidence that you will recover from problems *when* and not *if* they happen.

The best time to start caring for your nervous system is at birth and the second-best time is now. No one can ever 'fix' you because life is a dynamic, changing experience. Medication can trick your brain into believing the painful problem has gone, but the damage continues unless you do something about the cause of the pain. A hormone replacement medication is temporary, as the imbalance returns as soon as you stop taking the pill. It is your body that does the healing and the hard work and not the person or pill that comes from the outside. After all, a personal trainer can give you the tools to get fit, but they can't do the exercise for you. They don't sit with you 24 hours a day, grabbing the biscuits from your hand while persuading you to do a workout. You have to do that for yourself!

When you allow the natural cleverness of your body to correct itself, this is the closest to a fix you can get. However there will always be that process of damage followed by recovery. Your body heals itself from the inside out. This is why Chiropractors have a saying that we can't take away what's *wrong* with you, but maximise what's *right* within you.

HEALTH KEY

The only way to take darkness out of a room is to turn on a light

Reclaiming 'normal'

I remember the day two new mums arrived at my office, each with a 4-month-old baby for me to check. Sarah was telling me how concerned she was that her daughter hadn't pooed in a week. The other woman, Laura commented "I have the opposite problem, mine won't stop pooing all the time, because he still wakes up every 2 hours to feed." Both children the same age, one producing seemly endless dirty nappies while the other hadn't had one for a week. Both mums questioning what was normal. This is what happens when we confuse what is 'common' in life as we know it, with what is the 'normal' way your body was designed to work.

Sarah had been to the GP with her constipated baby who told her it was "common for breast fed babies not to poo for up to 10 days". This is because the doctor meets breastfed babies who are struggling to pass bowel movements on a regular basis. It is *common* but is it *normal*? It is more natural for humans of any age to pass stools once or twice per day. A 4-month-old child is taking in a lot of milk as it feeds regularly to grow, so you would expect them to poo several times a day.

On the other hand, Laura thought her baby might be pooing too often because he was still waking every 2 hours to feed. I had to reassure her this was normal. In nature it makes sense that babies wake regularly to feed, not just because they are growing rapidly, but it is an important way of getting more skin-to-skin contact with mum. This regulates the baby's heart rate, breathing, temperature and hormone levels. While it has now become *common* for babies to be expected to sleep for extended periods at this age, this isn't strictly *normal,* as it's not as nature designed.

I would like to re-claim the word *normal* for our health. I would like normal to mean when something happens which corresponds with having a healthy nervous system. For example, having a temperature when you are sick and babies falling asleep on the breast (it's how they develop hormones for their sleep/wake cycle). For me, 'normal' means to be as nature intended, rather than what usually happens. I want you to know that it's not *normal* to have consistent indigestion, allergies, tiredness or back ache. These are all signs of a nervous system which is struggling to work at its best.

When you confuse what's *common* or *usual* with what's *normal* or *healthy*, it makes it easy to look at someone who has more health problems that you do and believe you are well. Compared to them, you are well. However, if you look at how your body was designed to be, or how you would like it to be, how do you compare then? Normalising poor health makes everyone accept 'less than'. If you choose to focus on the next rung of the ladder, where an even better level of health awaits, the people around you become inspired into action. When this happens on a community level, you get to redefine normal.

HEALTH KEY

In health, normal means *as nature intended,* in which case just because something is common, it doesn't make it normal

Why resilience is key

The Ginkgo Biloba tree has existed for more than 200 million years and is a symbol of power and longevity. One tree alone can live for a thousand years. The gingko leaf has also come to represent adaptability and resilience because they have developed resistance to fire and two gingko trees even survived the nuclear bombs of Hiroshima.

I have a tattoo of the gingko leaf on my left wrist as it reminds me to have courage, resilience and strength throughout my life. I chose it as the emblem for my Chiropractic office because your nervous system is what gives you resilience to the stressors in life. Just as the branches of a tree must be able to bend and flex in the wind without breaking, your nervous system needs resilience to deal with stress otherwise a symptom will emerge. When you build resilience, you swap your small kitchen sink for a deep, wide sink with more capacity for stress.

Your body is also highly adaptable as it constantly responds to the world around you. An adaptation takes your body away from its original state. It can happen structurally, as in posture or having your leg in a cast to heal a broken bone. Or, it can be a negative thought process or some emotional stress. Being adaptable is healthy and important for us in the short term. However, when an adaptation happens for a long time, it becomes a *compensation.* This is a new habit which your brain begins mistaking for the 'new normal' and begins to affect your body in ways you hadn't planned. Like the client who didn't sit for 3 years, his ability to compensate for the bulge in his disc affected his family life, work, hobbies, weight and ultimately his quality of life. Adaptations that become habit eventually reduce your ability to deal with stressors in a healthy way, because they go against the natural cleverness of your body.

In the short term, having a resilient and adaptable nervous system will safeguard you against stressors you can't control. However, if there are too many stressors at once, or if they go on for too long, your body will enter the chemical state of stress which causes your health to be lost. Unfortunately, the longer your body stays in stress, the more stress builds within your system because it is no longer in a healing, renewing state. Now you need to increase your health-building behaviours and send a signal to your body that it is safe to move out of stress. As everything inside you is connected, a stressed state reinforces more stress in the same way that creating a relaxed, restorative state will allow healing to happen.

HEALTH KEY

Life doesn't get easier or more forgiving, we get stronger and more resilient

Do not fear the healing crisis

For me, Chiropractic only made sense once I had looked beyond the mechanics of the body and saw the bigger picture. There were times at the beginning of my career when I couldn't explain why one person had a negative reaction to an adjustment while another seemed to get better quickly. If they had the same mechanical problem, and I did the same therapy to each of them, what was the difference? My years studying neurology (how the brain and body are intricately connected and how the nervous system reacts to different situations) explained everything. Suddenly, everything fell into place and made sense. I can't unsee that and it hasn't let me down since. I can't predict what outcome someone will have from having an adjustment, because every nervous system is unique. What I can always trust is that the natural intelligence of the body knows what it is doing, even if it doesn't do what we expect.

The term 'healing crisis' really refers to the times when your health seems to get worse before it gets better. I find that people who have been under high levels of physical, chemical or emotional stress for many years are more likely to experience a healing crisis. Arguably these people will benefit from making health changes more than anybody else, but unless they understand why this is happening, they are quite likely to stop the change because they fear things are getting worse. When your nervous system is under a lot of strain, it is like a bowl of water that is already full to the brim. Now, any change in the nervous system, even if it is designed to help ease it, will temporarily cause the water to spill over the top. This is the healing crisis and in terms of your symptoms, things will often seem to get worse. Over time however, as stress is released from the nervous system, the water level goes down and leaves space, or capacity for change.

So how can you help ease this process? Keep the bowl of water in your mind for a moment and imagine filling it with ice cubes. These ice cubes represent the lifestyle stress that you carry around every day. As you know, the more cubes you have, the higher the water level rises. By making changes to your lifestyle to reduce your stress, you are effectively taking ice cubes out of your bowl and allowing the water level to drop. When you create extra capacity for stress in your life, it puts you in a strong place to deal with the stress of healing and change. Being kind to your body and giving it plenty of rest will help your body navigate through a healing crisis.

HEALTH KEY

The natural intelligence of the body knows what it is doing, even if it doesn't do what we expect

Always remember, healing takes time

I used to like jazzing up the water in my office to encourage more people to drink a glass when they came in. However, because I was closed for 3 days over the weekend, the herbs I bought to flavour the water kept dying. I would usually think to water them only as I was leaving on a Monday evening and these herbs were often wilted and wouldn't survive more than a couple of weeks.

When I did give the plants light and water again, what happened? Did they immediately spring back bright and green before my eyes? Well, that would have saved me a fortune in buying new plants. But once back in their ideal environment, they took time to recover and regrow. I didn't go overboard throwing in plant feeder and tying the wilting stems to a stick to make them perk up more quickly – I gave them what they needed and allowed nature to take its course.

The same is true in your body. Even when you are doing everything to restore your health, healing takes time. Throwing more at it won't make it happen any quicker. This is because it takes time for your cells to die-off and grow back new. It takes time and repetition for your better posture to become a habit. It takes time to get to a point where your health is fully restored and you have energy to explore your purpose.

The best way for you to uncover your full potential is to give yourself time. Sadly, we are under so much pressure to act now, decide now, buy now, we forget that we still have the luxury of time. That we have the freedom to choose to wait and let nature take its course. There is always the opportunity to try something else, however when we don't give ourselves enough time to heal, we mistakenly think we can't heal or improve without outside help. I recommend giving yourself 6-12 months with any approach to give your body time to change and restore. Remember that any kind of change affects your whole system and it takes time for the system to adapt.

HEALTH KEY

Just like going on a diet, or starting out at the gym, anything that requires physical change, like healing, takes time

Your wheel of health

My daughter is now 5 years old and still likes to wake me multiple times in the night, just to check-in for a quick cuddle. Sometimes my sleep is consistently interrupted for days and I wake up tired grumpy. Because of this I skip my morning meditation and workout, preferring a big breakfast for an energy boost. These are the days I just feel like eating biscuits on the sofa. Like the wheel on a bike, when a key area of your health – like sleep, the food you're eating, emotional challenges – gets out of balance, it knocks all the other areas off course. This is your wheel of health and it's a useful way to start seeing the bigger picture of how every area of your life influences another.

Health isn't a fixed destination: sadly, you can't just get there and relax. Every day you make choices and things happen that you can't control. Your body and nervous system respond accordingly. Every element of your health affects the others. A physical problem, especially if it comes with pain, will make you mentally tired and frustrated and drain your energy. Now you are more likely to introduce chemical stress through drugs, alcohol, caffeine or sugary foods so you can keep going. When one element is challenged, every part of your life is affected.

The opposite is also true. You exercise and feel great - physically strong and mobile while your brain releases lovely chemical endorphins to boost your mood. It's easier to say no to the unhealthy food choices and because you are physically tired, you sleep well. When you become aware of your wheel getting out of balance, it's easier to bring yourself back on course. By doing this, you are consistently moving towards your globetrotting dreams and away from a care home.

I find that days I wake up groggy and tired are the ones it's most important to get some exercise in early, even though I don't feel like doing it. The exercise will boost my energy, so my lack of sleep isn't such an issue. I know tiredness is making me crave unhealthy snacks, so I'll make sure I choose something more nutritious. As you begin to anticipate and adjust for the imbalances in your wheel, disruptions in one area begin to have less impact on the quality of your day.

With a little reflection on the physical, chemical and emotional elements of your health wheel, you will see which area to focus on that will have the biggest impact on your quality of life right now. I'll give you a little clue – it's usually the area you've been avoiding!

HEALTH KEY

Health isn't a fixed destination. Every day you make choices and things happen outside your control, you will always need to course correct

Chapter 3: Reaching Your Full Potential

The opportunity to experience something new has always appealed to me and I'm also quite impulsive. That's probably why I ended up climbing Mount Kilimanjaro with a client and later agreeing to go on a 4-day weekend in the countryside after a last-minute invitation from a stranger. I like to say yes to new things!

The weekend was hosted by a man called Philip McKearnon who is a life coach and mentor. The idea was to take time to reflect and take stock of our lives. Honestly, I found the experience emotionally challenging as I tend to prefer looking to the future, rather than reflecting on my past. On the last day, Philip asked us to do something he called 'free dreaming' where you draw a picture of your ideal life. He asked that we set aside our current commitments and responsibilities and draw as if anything were possible. I drew a picture of mountains, living with my family surrounded by nature and enjoying flexibility in both my time and what I did each day. "Uh oh, I thought, this doesn't look anything like the life I have now."

At the time I owned a busy and successful Chiropractic office with a good family life full of hobbies and friends. I certainly wasn't unhappy. But this weekend of reflection showed me the life I had created, wasn't what I craved deep down for my future. I had become swept up in various commitments and rhythms and unless I acted, I would continue to be propelled towards a different future. Over the next 2 years, I thought about this a lot and eventually decided to sell our established business and beautiful home to move back to my native Scotland. We found a house where we could look out onto mountains and began to get used to a completely different pace of life, and with the global pandemic, a different world.

Living in a house surrounded by nature gives me an immense feeling of calm that I just didn't feel when I lived in a town. This mental and emotional ease has helped me make better food choices, exercise regularly and show up differently at work and in my relationships at home. Our downtime is less busy so we have more time to be in nature, which makes us appreciate the life we have chosen. By changing my surroundings, I feel have created so much positive momentum in our lives. While we were healthy and happy before, this has moved us to a new level, one we didn't know existed, because we had been afraid to look beyond what we knew.

You don't have to be unhappy or dissatisfied with the life you have now, to benefit from creating more health for your future. You deserve to experience the best life possible and it's fun to explore how much more health and happiness you have to uncover.

HEALTH KEY

You don't have to be unhappy or dissatisfied with the life you have now, to benefit from creating more health for your future

Creating strong foundations

It was Don and Brandi MacDonald, my Chiropractic colleagues and mentors, who developed what they called 'the hierarchy of vitality' to illustrate how learning to put your health first will shift how you relate to the world around you. The reality is a bit more complicated than this, because life and health don't work in such a straight-forward way.

At the base of the hierarchy is restoring normal movement in the body. This is how the brain gets woken up and stimulated to make change. The brain then moves into the 'interrupted' phase, where it is getting new information from the spine but hasn't sorted out what to do with it yet. As new healthier patterns and habits form, your body and brain take these on as their new normal, until the nervous system is re-organised into working at its best. This means you now have a strong body and brain connection and that you feel trust in your body and health. Since there is now nothing to preoccupy your brain about what's happening inside you, you are able to begin to look outside of yourself more often. Able to reach out to those people around you in your family, community or even the world. Discovering your purpose is about figuring out what you are on this planet to achieve. That might be to raise strong, healthy, happy children or it might be to become the next amazing pro-golfer, writer, astronaut or anything you can think of.

Taking care of your physical body and health ultimately allows you to reach your full potential and find your purpose. It is much easier to unlock all your creative potential when you are thriving. Of course, some of us have health challenges which mean our version of 'thriving' is quite different to other people's. This isn't about copying a mythical blueprint of the 'best human body', but about uncovering the best version of you. Just as health comes out from the inside, so do happiness and potential.

The hierarchy of vitality is also a useful way of showing how health is a key foundation for the life that you want to achieve. You can build the most expensive, beautiful hotel in the world and have everyone you respect and admire want to stay there, but if the foundation isn't strong, the building, no matter how beautiful it is on the outside, can collapse. Creating a strong foundation for you to build a life, begins with your health, and good health begins with understanding and supporting your nervous system.

HEALTH KEY

Taking care of your physical body and health ultimately allows you to reach your full potential

Living and thriving – what's the difference?

On holiday in Portugal, I noticed how lush and green the plants were, despite the ample sunshine. Some days were so hot that I struggled to walk distances I normally find easy, seeking out shade and water instead. How then, did the greenery appear so lush and thriving when I was dried out and exhausted?

All over the park and well-kept streets the plants were being constantly maintained by a network of hosepipes, each pricked with thousands of tiny holes to allow water to be delivered to the plants as needed. This is how they could thrive despite the relentless heat of the Portuguese summer.

When a plant doesn't get the right balance of water and sunlight, it wilts. The first sign we notice that conditions aren't quite right is this wilting. The plant is not dead, but it's not as alive as it could be. A lot of human beings walk around in a wilted state – hunched shoulders, aches and pains, indigestion, constipation, barely enough sleep. Things are not so bad they think they need to ask for help but nor do they leap out of bed filled with energy, ready to seize the day.

This is the difference between living and thriving – thriving means that the organism (yourself, or a plant) is working to the best of its ability, filled with life and potential. Thriving bears fruit. When the system is out of balance, the organism begins to wilt – to live with less than its full growth and potential. It isn't dying, but there is a lack of life, meaning it will never achieve its fullest potential.

My biggest frustration of 20 years in healthcare in the UK is the "keep calm and carry on" attitude many of us still have. While I admire our stoicism as a nation, when it comes to our health and life potential, putting up with the status quo and carrying on isn't helping anybody: least of all, ourselves. I'm dismayed to think of the millions of people who could be enjoying a more fulfilled and longer life, helping each other and potentially making great changes. Carrying on will never lead you to thrive and it might even keep you in 'barely surviving' state. Like a plant given only just enough water to keep it alive, the 'make do with what you have' approach should not be applied to your health.

I believe what thriving means in your life, is unique to you. You may want to be the best parent, friend, sibling or colleague you can be. You might want to change the world through sporting achievements or the work that you do. You may simply want to lead an easy life, be able to travel and have the time and money to do what you love, with people who love you. All of these things become easier when you are thriving, not just living. And you deserve to have them.

> HEALTH KEY
>
> If you do what you need, you are living. If you do what you want, you are thriving

Your values matter

A value is a belief, a mission or a philosophy that is meaningful. Whether we are consciously aware of them or not, each one of us has values that we live our life by. You may value hard work, having nice things, travel, family or free time. There are no right or wrong values but knowing what yours are makes it easier to know whether you are thriving in your life and can help inspire change. For example when I realised how important it was for me to live around nature and mountains, this motivated me to push through the scary process of re-locating my family.

Knowing your values will help you to cut through a lot of the noise that you hear in the media and advertisements. Things which promise a 'quick fix', or 'low fat' and 'healthy' foods which are full of chemicals and high in sugars. Working and living in ways which match your values not only helps you to be happier and more content in your life, it reduces stress. Beginning to notice and honour your own value system can have a significant impact in your overall health. Living to our values is an important part of maintain our spiritual and moral wellbeing.

Businesses, people and places which reflect our values will make us feel more comfortable than those which don't. If you've ever found yourself liking a new person or a place without knowing exactly why, they are probably reflecting some of your own values back at you. In the same way, feeling 'something is off here, but I don't know what it is', can be a sign that your values are not being matched.

The ideas in this book are based on certain assumptions:

- Your body is part of nature
- Your body has natural or in-built cleverness (innate intelligence)
- Your body is a group of systems which are all interconnected, with each part affecting the others

- When you are healthy, you will have a friendly and trusting relationship with your body and generally the world around you

These statements reflect the values of someone who is vitalistic (life cannot be explained solely in terms of material, measurable things), naturalistic, holistic and humanistic. These are my values and reflect how I see the world.

The opposite to these ideas would be:

- Your body is separated from nature
- Everything related to your body can be explained in physical terms, the body has no intelligence or soul
- Your body is an unrelated collection of independent parts and is best understood by looking at the smallest possible part
- My own methods and points of view are more important to me than the wishes or opinions of others

These statements reflect the values of someone who is mechanistic (focusses on the physical parts and disregards natural intelligence), trusts manmade products and ideas over nature, and prefers to assess a system by looking at its smallest possible part.

These value systems don't have to be in complete opposition to each other: as a Chiropractor, I always measure and consider the mechanics of the body as part of my assessment. Clients often come with one primary concern and it's my job to show them how it is related to other things that are happening in their body. I love to see them make the connections for themselves and to begin to see their body in a new way. None of these values are better than others, however your experience of life is better when you can live in ways that align with your values.

HEALTH KEY

Knowing your values makes it easier to find the best ways to allow yourself to thrive

It's not what you do, it's how you do it

Like survival vs. thriving, each of the values has its extremes and you can sit anywhere between them in different areas of your life. One of the great benefits of recognising your values is that it makes decision making much easier. If you develop a headache, you already know if you are the type of person who wants to take a pill or if you would rather uncover the cause. Your values help you decide where to shop, what to buy, the products you use on your body and to clean your home and even the types of clothing you prefer.

Your value system will affect how you take care of your health. We are all used to hearing the warning "Don't catch a cold" but in reality the common cold virus is around us all the time. You don't actually *catch* the cold virus but *succumb* to it when your immune system drops below a certain level, usually as a result of stress. This is why you often feel run down when you've had a lot going on in your life and you haven't been able to take care of your health as you would like.

If you feel as though you are developing a runny nose, sore throat and feel tired, what do you do? A naturalist will choose a warm drink of honey and lemon over a pouch of cold and flu remedy from the chemist. A vitalist will acknowledge that they are rundown because they have been 'burning the candle at both ends' and trust this is their body telling them to stop and take a rest. A holist will respect this message and try to slow down and reduce their overall stress, rather than try to fight the symptoms so they can carry on regardless. A humanist will be gentle towards themselves and not feel any pressure to quickly get back to work or the gym.

When you come down with a cold, do you see it as a warning to slow down before things get worse or, you can see it as an inconvenient blip that the wonders of modern medicine can erase from your life quickly and easily? How you experience and manage your common cold is a great of showing your value system.

Noticing and honour your own value system can have a significant impact in your overall health as living to our values is an important part of maintain our spiritual and moral wellbeing.

HEALTH KEY

How you experience and manage your common cold is a great of showing your value system

Environment matters more than you may think

The environment matters. We care about it a lot and increasingly choose to spend more money on environmentally friendly products and ethical goods. But how much thought do you give to your personal environment? The elements which surround you? When we are in living in the right environment, we thrive. This doesn't just mean that health and life are improved but it also allows us to move up that hierarchy of vitality, so we can generate the energy and finances we need to invest in what we care about and make a difference in the wider world. When we live in an environment that drains us, the opposite is true.

A fish living in a pond where the water is dirty, stagnant, and filling up with the excretions of other animals, will begin to suffer. It won't grow to its full potential or live as long as it could. No matter what supplements, food or care you now give to that fish, it won't become any healthier. A fish living in a toxic pond cannot thrive without its environment being changed.

Health comes from the inside out, but our surroundings still affect us deeply. Just like the fish, if your live your life in a chemical, emotional or physical 'toxic pond' you won't be able to reach your full potential. Living in a relationship filled with unhappiness, frustration or uncertainty creates emotional stress which stops us from being whole and healthy no matter how hard we diet or how often we exercise. A work environment where we never seem to be good enough or get enough done, creates the belief that we aren't good enough, and our choices and health suffer as we stop believing we are worth the effort. Drinking alcohol or taking drugs to numb the discomfort of our daily lives, begins to rot our insides and affect how we think and act. When the environment you live in isn't serving you, the benefit you will gain from making positive health choices will be limited.

I remember listening to a call-in radio show which asked people if they'd ever noticed their health improve after changing their job or relationship? Hundreds of people got in touch and one man described how, after ending 20 years in an unfulfilling marriage, his diabetes and heart problems appeared to improve almost overnight. His emotional environment was serious impacting his physical health. Once that stress was relieved his body was then able to return to normal physiology and heal as it was designed to.

Nature has great bounce-back given the right environment. I saw this first-hand when I rescued battery hens and added them to my spoiled free-range brood. The birds we collected were missing feathers and their combs, instead of being red, shrivelled and bright, were white and flaccid. Their skin was pale and they just sat, hardly moving. Within 48 hours of living with fresh air, space and stimulating surroundings, a red colour began to appear in their combs, their legs became stronger and their natural inclination to scratch and peck kicked in. I felt humbled at how quickly nature could recover when given the right environment. Is there something in your environment that is holding you back from reaching your full potential?

HEALTH KEY

You cannot thrive in an environment that isn't nourishing you

Making friends with your body

Most of us are pretty good at judging how our body looks or feels at a given time, but we don't consider it as a source of energy and joy. In fact, most of us are disconnected from our bodies. I don't necessarily mean this in an emotional way (although that certainly happens) but on a physical level. Sit for a second with your eyes closed and imagine me placing an object in the palm of your hand. It can be anything: a pair of scissors, a spoon, a fluffy toy. Without being able to see it or feel all over it your brain doesn't stand much of a chance knowing what it is. That's because your brain lives in a dark cave we call the skull and is fully reliant on information from the body to make sense of the world around us.

Another way I show this to people, is by asking them to march on the spot with their eyes closed for 60 seconds and then measure how far they stray from the spot where they started. In a decade of carrying out this experiment with every new client, I have never tired of seeing the surprise on their faces when they see how far they have moved while feeling like they were stood on one spot. In fact, I am now so experienced in this, that has come to be one of the most reliable indicators of how well the messages are travelling from body to brain and from brain to body. There is a disconnection here which tells me that

that person is probably very unaware of how well their body is doing, because they simply can't connect with it.

Often, these people don't spend much time thinking about their bodies or may have grown to distrust them ("I hadn't done anything differently, I simply leaned forward and my back went on me"). With everything else that is going on in the world, it seems that taking time to tune into our bodies is the last thing we have time for. However, what if was the most important habit we could form that would make navigating our stressful lives that much easier?

Since being on this journey of health and self-discovery, I have been amazed by how much the Chiropractic philosophy of natural intelligence, holism and connection echoes around the world. Deepak Chopra says: "This is a kind of disconnect that undermines the body. The main thing that is needed in renewal of the physical body is to reconnect with it." When we reconnect with our body, we can enjoy a more friendly relationship with it. This is a much more stable and comfortable place for us to experience the world.

In her book, *The Body is Not an Apology,* Sonya Renée Taylor explains that you don't need to strive for more things or accumulate more things, but that you need to get rid of whatever is getting in your way of tapping into your natural purpose or greatness. This could be looking a certain way, achieving financial or social status or buying into a negative culture of comparison and competition. She says that self-acceptance is to make peace with where you are now, whereas what she terms *radical self-love* compels you to take steps towards making the best choices for you, regardless of the status quo.

For many of us, the first step to reaching our full potential begins with our health and lifestyle choices. By honouring the body you have been given and nourishing it with exercise, food, rest and respect you can begin to move your way up the hierarchy of health and explore your potential. By putting health first, you will create more mental headspace and physical energy to channel into improving life for others as well as yourself.

HEALTH KEY

When we reconnect with our body, we can enjoy a more friendly relationship with it. This is a much more stable and comfortable place for us to experience the world

It's time to put yourself first

I was brought up to believe that putting others before yourself made you a good person. However, there's a problem with this, at least there is when you *always* put others' needs before your own. Being there for other people or even being really dedicated to your work is like breathing out: it takes energy from you. But you can't exhale oxygen without taking time to breathe it back in. Self-care is like you taking a deep breath in, so you can exhale again. Putting someone else's needs before your own is fine in the short term, but it takes energy to be there for other people. It's impossible to sustain that energy if you don't take time to re-charge.

When it comes to your health, putting your needs at the top of your priority list is the best way to make sure you can support friends and family when they need you. It's also important that the self-care you choose fits who you are as a person. You will get much more overall benefit exercising outdoors if you enjoy being in nature than if you sign up to a gym. When your self-care strategy suits you and you enjoy doing it, it's much easier to sustain.

It's also useful to recognise which habits are the most important for you to keep healthy. A man's body is designed to build lean muscle and stay active. When he stops exercising, he loses his energy and drive while his body releases more of the hormone oestrogen and begins to lay fat in areas that you would associate with a woman. Regular exercise is the one of the best ways for men to avoid depression. Women on the other hand, are designed for emotional connection – we talk. Without a community or friend to relate to, women become isolated and open to depression. When time is short or life gets busy, knowing which behaviours are most important for your wellbeing can help you prioritise.

Taking care of yourself is the *first* step in being able to take care of other people, *not* the last. Anytime you find yourself struggling to make time for your health, it helps to focus on the benefit of doing the activity, the goodness it will bring you, rather than the inconvenience of making time for it in that moment.

Having a strong, balanced, healthy nervous system allows you to:

- Have the freedom to do as you please: travel, exercise, take on new challenges and push yourself to reach new goals
- Feel energetic and motivated to get involved with things you're passionate about
- Be able to enjoy your family and be there for them
- Do everything you've dreamed of doing when you retire

Over time I have come to realise that what I value most in my life is freedom. Freedom to have choice about what I do with my life, and the basic building block of freedom and choice, is health. When I am healthy, I can say 'yes' to everything that excites me. I can travel, meet physical challenges and rise to the challenge of running a business while having a young family without feeling overwhelmed. My good health and capacity to handle stress means I don't have to choose between them. I also know that as a parent, showing my child that self-care is important, will mean that she learns it is important for her too. When my daughter grows up and has a busy job and children of her own, I know she is more likely to make time to care for herself if I have shown her how to do it. For you to create all the possibilities you want in your future, you may need to start putting yourself at the top of your priority list.

> HEALTH KEY
>
> Putting yourself first allows you to be a better provider and support for others

Healthy Families Need Healthy Role Models

Tonight on my social media I read, "Most parents are willing to die for their kids but very few are willing to live healthy lives for them." Whoever wrote this seems to suggest that parents don't care about creating a healthy lifestyle for their children. In my experience, most parents are desperate for their children to lead healthy lives, but this is not as easy as it sounds. Keeping our children healthy is time-consuming, expensive and often means going against the status quo. You want to give your child access to lots of fabulous out of school activities, hobbies, education and fun. But before you know it, you are rushing around every day after school and on weekends, grabbing meals in the car. Some families will need to reduce the quality of food they buy, to have more money to spend on hobbies and sports.

As parents we want to give our children the best, and this good intention can mean the whole family is lacking that all-important need for downtime and relaxation. In a world which demands so much of parents, while giving them little support, we can easily become unhealthy role models for our children as the stress of 'keeping up' begins to affect our own health. Creating healthy habits in our children seems clear-cut when you glance at it but in reality, it is more easily said than done.

In her book *The Gifts of Imperfect Parenting*, Brené Brown explains that our children will do what we show them and not what we tell them. This means that I can tell my daughter to make time for herself, take exercise, spend money on food which nourishes her and get to bed on time. But if what she sees is me sacrificing my own self-care time for others, quickly grabbing food on the go and staying up late to tidy, watch TV or whatever else, this is what she will do herself. To create health for the entire family, more parents need to go against the cultural grain of providing endless opportunities for their children and instead have the confidence to press pause on the business and focus on taking care of every member of the family, themselves first.

Living the un-doctored life, taking responsibility and action for our health isn't easy. It's hard to go against the cultural flow. It is so tempting to do what everyone else is doing, cross our fingers and hope for the best. Reducing the number of after-school activities your child enjoys so that you can have time to do your own things, is going against the grain.

We all want our children to do better than we did: be healthier, happier and more fulfilled. I wholeheartedly believe that this can only happen when we show them how to do it. How to swim against the cultural tide of never having enough and never putting ourselves or our health first. The best way to create a healthy lifestyle for your children is to show them what it looks like.

HEALTH KEY

If you didn't come from a healthy family, you can make sure a healthy family comes from you

Starting them young

As a Chiropractor, I have a special interest in caring for children and have had the privilege of supporting many young people over the years. There are many reasons for Chiropractors to check the spines of children and not just adults. The central nervous system, that most important highway of information flowing through the body has a lot of work to do in those growing years. Think of all the ways children develop from birth to adulthood. Doesn't it make sense to check and support that system as it experiences the periods of greatest change in its life?

One of the most important windows for child development is before 3 years old because this is when their nervous system finishes developing. Beyond this age, our children go on to face a host of physical, chemical and emotional stressors as part of their everyday lives: time spent on screens, processed food and the pressures of social media to name a few. Just as in adults, an imbalance of stress in a child's life can cause interrupted sleep, mood swings, difficulty processing emotion, fluctuating energy (over or under energised), tummy upsets and a tendency to catch every bug and illness going. You will see the signs of a stressed nervous system even in young children if you know where to look.

Having your child grow up under Chiropractic care teaches them early that taking care of their health is something that they should do. By forming this habit from birth, your child is much more likely to continue to be interested in their own health and wellbeing as they grow into adulthood. It will be natural for them to practice self-care, exercise and eat well so they can go on to live long and happy lives. Having their nervous system checked should be just as normal to your child as visiting the dentist, and spines are even more precious than teeth as they can't be replaced!

> HEALTH KEY
>
> Having their nervous system checked should be just as normal to your child as visiting the dentist

Make time for rest

Growing up, we didn't specifically talk about health in my family, it just wasn't part of our everyday conversation. Diet and healthy eating was my greatest challenge and it has taken a decade of small and consistent change for me to really feel confident in my own health and have a friendly relationship with my body. In the next chapter, I'll share my story with you including all the tools that helped me along the way. Before I do however, it's important we talk about rest. Keeping your nervous system in balance might sound like a challenge because it is. That said, rest is something you can add into your life right now, for free.

It's physically and mentally easy once you get into it and really quite enjoyable. Taking regular rest is a wonderful way to reduce stressors and listen to the natural cleverness in your body.

I would guess that so far, resting has not been the at the top of your list of priorities. There is so much we need to *do* in our lives – deal with family, work, make time to exercise, shop, eat, tidy and organise, that you never think the most helpful thing you could do might be nothing at all. But your body's ability to heal and restore is much greater when you make time to rest. Hipprocates said "Doing nothing is sometimes a good remedy" and he was right. Studies show that taking time to rest regularly, increases healing, productivity and concentration which are all important for a good life. Making space in your life for rest shows self-compassion and respect and can help fulfil your spiritual needs. Rest gives you more energy in your day and it allows your body to physically restore, so muscles can re-grow stronger.

It's important to say that having fun on your days off work is not the same as resting, as most hobbies demand some physical or mental effort. Have you ever come back from holiday and thought you could do with a holiday to recover from the one you just took? Resting is restorative. Breaks, holidays and days off can be just as stressful to your body as a full-on work day, unless you make time to rest. By all means go to the gym or take a long walk, but also make time to just be. To get bored and do nothing and let yourself be restored.

HEALTH KEY

Taking regular rest is a wonderful way to reduce stressors and tune into the natural cleverness in your body

Chapter 4: How to Change Your Health

"Can you imagine yourself in 10 years if instead of avoiding the things you know you should do, you actually did them every single day – that's powerful"
Jordan Peterson

The motivation to write this book comes from my own personal experience of learning to trust my body. Monday 1 August 2011 was my first day as a newly qualified Chiropractor and I was so overweight and unfit, I struggled to walk up the big hill leading to my first job. Panting and sweaty, I arrived to meet my muscly, lean 40-year old boss who was an energetic Chiropractor and family man. I remember feeling so intimidated by how sorted his life seemed that I felt afraid to ask questions. I genuinely believed I could never be as healthy as he was because I had so far to go. It made me question whether I could really *be* a Chiropractor, because surely, I needed to be healthy myself before I could help others do the same?

It took me nearly 18 months of working in that office before I found the motivation to drop one third of my body weight. It felt like the right time to make a change and I was ready to put in the effort. However, it's taken many years for me to make regular exercise a habit. Now, 10 years on and I finally pack my workout gear for a holiday, not just because I 'have to' but because I feel motivated to do some form of exercise every day. I have developed a simple morning routine of meditation, exercise and food that allows me to enjoy life while taking care of my body. Today, I could walk back into my first associate position and feel as though I fit in. But it has taken a decade of small, consistent changes for healthy habits to become part of my natural routine.

Getting healthy isn't about quick-fix solutions or false promises, it's about making small, consistent changes which fit naturally into your life. During my transformation there have been some huge highlights – feeling great in my wedding dress, completing several fire walks and my first half marathon to name a few. However, the reason I peel myself out of bed on these cold, dark Scottish mornings is not because I want the next big achievement. It's because I now cherish how it feels to have a friendlier relationship with my body: to protect it from stress, nourish it, rest it and pay it attention. In return it has rewarded me with loads more energy and sharper concentration. I am a calmer, more easy-going wife and parent who can stop and be present with my daughter. I am more aware of the people and the world around me and this has made me a better Chiropractor. In a time of great uncertainty and restricted opportunities, keeping myself well has given me focus and allowed me to reach out to others.

I have also learned how to balance my stress, to stop over-filling my diary and I am working on being okay with rest days. I enjoy the idea that continuing to work on my health is a lifelong project that never ends, but rewards me constantly along the way. I am also protecting myself for the future. If I want to spend retirement hiking around the world, shopping and enjoying myself, I don't want any health issues getting in the way of all the fun I plan to have. In this chapter, I will share the 3 key tools I used to create change in my life. Whichever part of your life you choose to work on first, you can use it to help form a new healthy habit. I would recommend only addressing one area of your life at a time, knowing that it will impact other areas too (this is your wheel of health).

The first step to making changes in your life is to let go of the idea that it's going to happen quickly, or all at once. The more you take easy, simple steps, the more likely you are to succeed. By changing just one small thing at a time, you will begin to create your own snowball effect in your life, where one positive change leads to another. Personal development coach Marc Allan has a wonderful mantra for change which I have stuck up on my wall to remind me to slow down and do it the right way. It reads: "In an easy and relaxed manner, in a healthy and positive way, in its own perfect time, I am..."

We live in a world which demands results tomorrow, but all these quick-fix solutions and fad diets lead you back to where you started. By taking it easy, going slow and allowing your body to change in its own perfect time, you can take consistent steps towards good health. Allow yourself to shift your focus beyond the next few days, into the months and years ahead, knowing that a small change today will slowly combine to create big change in the years to come.

My journey began when I started to experience the inner satisfaction of one small change – I found an eating plan which worked for my body and lifestyle so I was able to lose weight without it feeling like a punishment. More than the pleasure of looking better, the energy boost I experienced was amazing. I naturally craved more of the same and tried to include more habits that boosted this feeling and drop those that took my energy away. You may think creating a real long-term change is far beyond you but, how do you eat an elephant? Piece by piece. Once you realise how good it feels to make these small changes you'll get through them in your own perfect time.

HEALTH KEY

The first step to making changes in your life is to let go of the idea that it's going to happen quickly, effortlessly, or all at once

Making change happen

"Before you heal someone, ask him if he's willing to give up the things that make him sick" Hippocrates

---

The most important reason to make healthier lifestyle choices, much more than how good you want to look or even feel, is that healthy changes will support your nervous system and build your resilience against stress. This is how you can help secure your own dreams of a fulfilling and active older life.

The first step is to motivate yourself to prefer a healing lifestyle to a stressful one. The simplest way to do this is to implement a small change in your life that gives you a small feeling of, "Wow, that effort paid off, I feel good." Once this becomes a common feeling in your life, you will find yourself naturally wanting to re-create that sensation and adopting better lifestyle choices will start to happen on its own. I call this the 'positive snowball effect', as your good feeling and behaviour start to gain their own momentum in your life.

Creating change is simple, but it isn't easy. You should prepare yourself to deal with the frustration of slow change and the temptation to slip back to old habits or to go with the flow of those around you. Sometimes change is physically hard or emotionally painful. I found changing my eating habits brought up emotions from my childhood which I had forgotten about. A child of 2 hardworking parents, I would come home from school, eat a snack and then have a couple of hours to wait until teatime. Nothing wrong there, except my 8-year-old brain thought those 2 hours lasted for days and I began to experience anxiety around feeling hungry. In my adult life, I would keep myself constantly fed because I didn't enjoy the feeling of hunger and would eat until I was over-full because that made me feel safe. Untangling my childhood emotions around food was a big part of helping me successfully manage my eating. It's still hard, but understanding why it's hard helps me honour my body and health rather than my emotions around food.

HEALTH KEY

The first step is to make one small change that makes you feel good and encourages you to keep going

Change Isn't Comfortable

"To change is to think greater than how we feel... to act greater than the familiar feelings of the memorised self"
Joe Dispenza

One of the most important things you can do when you want to improve your health is to talk about it with others. Begin by asking your partner, "What do you think about my health and how I take care of myself?" By talking to close friends and family about how they see your health you can often get new insights. It also helps them to support you in changing. You may even inspire them to do it with you!

Talking about your health, even with the people you love, takes honesty and vulnerability. You may notice some resistance from inside yourself, especially if your friends or loved ones are scared about you making changes and how it might affect the dynamics of your relationship. Brené Brown developed 6 stages of an 'armouring up' thought process which happens in leadership situations, but it adapts very well into conversations around health too. Be aware of this negative thinking process which can stop you getting permission to change:

1. I haven't done a good enough job of taking care of myself.
2. If I admit I have a problem, I might look weak or someone might use it against me.
3. Why do I have to be the one who talks about it? No one else does.
4. I am not the unhealthiest person I know.
5. This isn't about helping me at all, this is about you trying to change me.
6. I'm actually okay with where I am right now.

Can you see how easy it is for your clever brain to convince you that you are okay as you are and you don't need to make a change? Remember, this process isn't about fixing what is *wrong* with you, it is about maximising everything that is *right* within you. You are discovering your full potential and knowing that *you* are the answer. This is a hard process and the more support you have, the more likely you are to succeed.

While the goal of all these changes is for you to have a friendlier relationship with your body, at first your body is likely to resist changes on a chemical level. For example, even though we know smoking is bad for our health, people still do it and struggle to give up. Anyone who has tried will tell you that the *routine* of smoking is very hard to break, which is why people have greater success when they go through the motions of pretending to smoke a fake cigarette. This is because their body is used to the hit of the feel-good hormone dopamine, even before they light up. By going through the motions with a fake cigarette, their brain will release some dopamine even without the nicotine hit. The same happens right before you crack open the biscuit tin when the kids have gone to bed or when you allow yourself a lie-in instead of getting up to do that workout.

Your body is so used to the regular pattern of hormones in your body, that if they suddenly change for some reason, your body sends a chemical signal to your brain saying "something's wrong, this doesn't feel right." Your body likes routine, even when it is bad for you. Being in a predictable state feels safer and more comfortable than change. Whenever you try to change that state, even though it is better for your health and body in the long term, you are likely to experience some resistance. I am now going to share with you 3 key concepts which I found to be the best tactics for overcoming my own resistance to change.

HEALTH KEY

Good health isn't about fixing what is *wrong* with you, it is about maximising everything that is *right* within you

Key to Change #1: The 5 Second Rule

Mel Robbins, author of *The 5 Second Rule* explains that one of the major obstacles to change, is overcoming the inner voice in your head that lists all the reasons *not* to do something. Think now of the first small change you would like to make that would have a positive impact on your wheel of health. It might be to wake up earlier each day so you have some time to yourself to exercise or to sit in quiet reflection. On that first morning, your alarm goes off and you wake up feeling groggy. Your inner voice says, "I want to stay in bed, I'm too tired, it's still dark, I didn't sleep well, I can still do this later…" it has a million reasons to excuse you from getting up earlier. So how can you overcome the resistance?

Mel's rule says that upon opening your eyes, before that inner dialogue even starts, you need to do 2 things: start counting backwards from 5 (in your head) and take

ACTION. You must physically move your body on the word "action". So, as soon as your alarm goes off, before your inner voice kicks in, you begin counting backwards "5,4,3,2,1" and STAND UP.

This tactic works because your brain can't count backwards and persuade you to stay in bed at the same time. It's impossible! By the time you've stopped counting, you're already standing up so you might as well get on with it. Mel suggests using this tool anytime you have something you need to do, but feel reluctant. It can be anything at all, like walking away from the fridge, making a phone call or signing up for a challenge. 5, 4, 3, 2, 1... Go!

I credit this little nugget as being the only reason I was able to make running a regular part of my life. Sometimes, I would have to use it multiple times even to get out of the house: countdown to get up out of bed, countdown to get dressed, countdown to get downstairs and shoes on. BIG countdown to leave the house. One cold, dark, rainy Saturday morning I had to use the 5 second rule at least 7 times to get myself out of the house and was already 3 miles into my run and my brain was *still* complaining about how I didn't want to be there. I remember thinking, "Why am I doing this to myself? Why am I making this run so miserable by focussing on how much I am not enjoying it?" This is when I discovered tactic number 2.

HEALTH KEY

The 5 second rule: "5,4,3,2,1.... Move your body"

Mel Robbins

Key to Change #2: Focus on the Benefit

My husband and I attended a live event with world-renowned life coach Tony Robbins. In an auditorium of 13,000 people in London, he asked everyone to put up their hands if they exercised at least 4 days a week. Around 10% raised their hands. He asked a few people sitting with their hands down why they didn't exercise at least 4 days every week. Most said they didn't have the time. "How many people here have 24 hours in their day?" Tony then asked. All 13,000 people raised their hands.

We all have the same opportunity for healthy lifestyle habits in our day, so why don't we all create the time for it? Very often it's because you are focussing on the *pain* of that change rather than the *benefit*. On that Saturday when I woke up for my run, I was thinking, "It's cold and wet out, I don't want to go. It will be so much nicer staying tucked up cosy in bed, I never have time for a lie-in." I am focussed on the downside of getting out in the pouring rain, rather than the good it will bring me. Tony suggests flipping these thoughts around to focus only on the benefit. For example, deciding to take a brisk 20 minute walk outside each lunchtime is a simple way to care for your physical and mental health. On day 1 you think, "I don't want to go out for a walk at lunchtime, it means moving from my desk and having more work to do later. My colleagues might think I'm not a hard worker." Are you likely to go out? Probably not. However, if you focussed on the benefits of a lunchtime walk: being able to enjoy a well-earned break, be more productive in the afternoon and get some extra steps in, are you more likely to go now?

Quite simply, when you only concentrate on the pain of the change, you are much less likely to do it. By focussing on all the benefits, you give yourself as much motivation as possible to create that change. Think about how your new habit will help you not just on the day, but once you have done it consistently in the future. How will you look? Feel? What will your energy be like? How much healthier and happy will you become?

I found that having all these benefits at the front of my mind was most useful when I was in a social situation which might cause me to skip a workout, drink alcohol when I hadn't intended to, or order the burger instead of the healthier option. I found that the little glow of achievement I had at sticking to my new habit lasted longer than the flash of pleasure that came from indulgence. Although I certainly chose the less healthy option quite a few times before figuring this out! When you make the right choice for your health on a regular basis, you begin to respect yourself more. Then tactic 3 helped me stick to my plans long enough to make it happen.

HEALTH KEY

"Focus on the benefits, rather than the pain"

Tony Robbins

Key to change #3: Commit for 30 days

I remember being about 10 years old, standing in the kitchen and putting my arms out to give my mum a hug. Instead of gathering me to her, she reached out and held a roll of fat around my middle. "When are we going to do something about this?" she asked. I never grew out of my 'puppy fat', I didn't enjoy exercise but I've always enjoyed food. So many times over the course of my life, I have tried to change my diet, mindset, exercise regime so that I could feel comfortable and proud of my body. Every time I tried and failed, I found it harder to want to try again. Deep down, I didn't believe that I could succeed. Today my body still doesn't always look exactly as I'd like, but I'm damn proud of it and everything it does for me.

It wasn't until I read *Girl, Stop Apologising* by Rachel Hollis that I realised how damaging all my failed attempts at creating new habits were to my self-esteem. Every time I quit after a few days, I was reinforcing the idea that I wasn't capable of creating lasting change. Rachel suggests that whatever has happened in your past sets your standard for 'normal'. This in turn, influences your self-worth. So if you intend to give up chocolate for a month but usually cave after 3 days, then 3 days becomes your standard. This in itself doesn't have a negative impact on your life, however somewhere in your subconscious you are creating and reinforcing the idea that you don't follow through on your intentions. This can have a negative impact on your self-esteem, even to the point where you stop trying.

After I read this, I found it helpful that each time I was tempted to 'quit' on myself I realised there was more at stake than a few extra calories, or a missed workout. I didn't want to break a promise to myself or commit to low standards. I am good at pushing myself at work: trying new things, agreeing to projects that scare me. I know that in some areas of my life, I can do hard things because frankly, I don't like to admit when I'm not up to something. When I started to tell myself that stopping something before trying it for 30 days meant I was quitting on myself, it gave me the motivation to keep going, where I could easily have given myself permission to stop.

The 30 days is important. Science shows that when we do something consistently for 30 days, it's much more likely to become a habit. It works whether you want to take up something, like having 20 minutes of mindfulness before bed, or take something out, like giving up fizzy drinks. After 30 days your body comes to expect the wave of calmness it has enjoyed with your mindfulness or forgotten what it's like to experience the sugar rush of the drinks. When you pour yourself a large glass of Coke after a month you might find it disgusting! Being consistent helps create positive change. Chances are, if you skip a mindfulness session after a month of practice, you will miss the calm it brings and make sure to do it the next day.

When it comes to creating new healthy habits, start with something that fits easily into your daily routine, so you maximise your chances of success. Fitting 20 minutes of exercise into your day is better than trying and failing to find an hour. Every new habit can be built on. By committing to the change for just 30 days, it feels more manageable, whereas "from now on" can feel daunting. In the same way, doing too much at once will create pressure and make you more likely to give up. By taking it easy, you can create positive momentum and build self-esteem around your new habit.

I found these 3 tools for change simple to use and they work well for me to this day. However, there are still days that I struggle to do all the 'right' things and give in to all my temptations. In the bigger picture however, these short periods of indulgence or laziness don't matter, so long as I keep re-balancing my wheel of health. Each day is a new day and a new opportunity to make good choices. Keep focussing on all the benefits your new lifestyle will bring you, both now and in the future. Delight in every small win until it becomes the habit you want it to be.

HEALTH KEY

Start with one small change which fits easily into your current lifestyle and commit to trying it each day for at least 30 days before stopping or adding something new

Give yourself a break

Whatever steps you take to create a better life for yourself, be gentle with your 'failures'. Despite all your best intentions, there will be times that you break commitments to yourself. There is space in life for an indulgent weekend or a few days without exercise, or a few late nights. Please, don't beat yourself up about it. Being aware that you have gone off track is a good sign and developing this awareness is an essential first step to creating change. When you do want to relax your healthy habits, do it *mindfully*. Enjoy every delicious cocktail, yummy treat or lie-in instead of a workout. Savour the chance to let it all go, for a set amount of time (you decide what that is), then pick yourself up and get back on track.

During my weight loss and later my half marathon training, I had to take breaks every few months. I felt it released the pressure of having to improve all the time and meant I didn't run out of motivation before I got to my goal. By starting your good habits exactly when you intend to, you are reinforcing to your subconscious that you are a person of your word: trustworthy, dedicated and in control. Anytime you have a slip, especially if you didn't intend to, use it as a learning opportunity. Notice how much more tired, unmotivated and sluggish you feel. This can be a powerful reminder of why you put in the hard work to be healthy.

We live in a world where everything happens instantly: next day delivery, instant credit, instant news, instant messaging. At the last general election, the results were called by the newsreaders before the polls had even closed. Never have we been less prepared to give people our time, including ourselves. Health and healing is not an instant result. True healing takes time and while it can feel frustrating, months or even a year of your life is not long in the context of your whole live.

In her book *The Beauty in All Things,* Elizabeth Gilbert introduced me to different concepts of time. There is the time that passes on this earth where mountains and seas form and is measured over millions of years. Moss, however, (yes that green stuff that grows on everything) has its own speed too, growing and retreating over decades. Much faster than mountain time but slow enough that the average person doesn't notice it. Then there is a human lifetime, which for the mountain and the moss passes in the blink of an eye. I find this idea comforting when I am feeling frustrated about time. Improving any area of your health means shifting your perspective away from instant gratification and towards gentle, rhythmic change.

You are the answer

The best place to start looking for inspiration for creating long-term health is in your wheel of health in response to what tends to push you out of balance most often. Adding habits that will support your physical, chemical and emotional wellbeing or stopping something which is damaging it. Classic areas are food, hydration, mindset, exercise, posture and sleep. Focussing on any one of these areas will create improvements in all of them. Usually you will instinctively know which area will help you the most and where you want to start. Every human on the planet is uniquely different and I don't believe in a 'one size fits all' approach to health or lifestyle choices.

My husband loves to spend his spare time in forests: building shelters, camping and cooking. A year ago, we did a foraging course together which completely changed my diet. We spent the morning foraging for various plants, seeds and berries to make a delicious lunch, and we were also provided with some freshly shot birds to prepare as the meat. They expected us to prepare the bird by hand but I couldn't do it. Perhaps the Chiropractor in me couldn't bear the idea of twisting and pulling the joint of the wings until they snapped off, I just couldn't. The man running the course turned to me and said, "If you can't prepare the food yourself, you probably shouldn't be eating it." I was inclined to agree.

From that day I decided to stop eating meat for a week to see what it was like. Writing this over one year later, I am yet to start eating it again. You see I found not eating meat not only better honoured my values, but it also matched my body. I discovered I had more energy, found it easier to maintain a healthy weight and never even missed it. It's the only 'diet' I've ever found easy to maintain, because it fits perfectly with my body. A few months in, my husband agreed to give up meat for a month to see if he preferred it too. He spent the whole month counting the days until he could eat meat again, his body really craved it. Now he eats much less meat and we only buy from our local butcher so we know about the wellbeing and health of the animals.

I don't believe there's such a thing as an ideal diet. I know many healthy people who follow diets which are high in fat or carbs or protein. Some eat meat, some have no dairy at all. I believe the key to a healthy diet for *you*, is to spend time tuning into your body and noticing how it responds. You know the basics: choose organic, remove processed food and chemicals, cook from fresh ingredients. The detail is up to you. A healthy diet is really a way of eating that supports your lifestyle. Your daily calories will depend on your exercise and goals and the make-up of your perfect diet is unique to your body and can change over time. Forget trying to do what works for other people because you are not other people.

Sometimes you will need the help of a professional to create the change you want, but there are hundreds of ways you can improve your health at home, for free, without any special qualifications. Just start listening to your body. The goal of self-care is to help minimise the physical, emotional and chemical stresses which come up in your life and negatively affect your nervous system. Prioritising self-care is important if you want your body to be healthy, active, full of energy and feel like a friendly place to live. I've included 10 simple self-care habits to help inspire you on your way, but there are many more.

If there is an area of your life where you know it is time for a big shift, or an area where you lack knowledge or confidence, seeking professional help will give you the support and accountability you need. I am a great believer in the concept of TEAM – together everyone achieves more. Whenever there is an area in my life that I want to improve, I find someone who is an expert in that area to show me the way. It is much easier for you to create healthy lifestyle habits when you work alongside a practitioner who is trained in the principles of good and lasting health. Find someone who shares your values, so you trust and feel comfortable with them.

HEALTH KEY

Every human on the planet is uniquely different. There is not a 'one size fits all' solution

Movement is life

Everyone knows that exercise is an essential part of keeping our bodies healthy. But did you know it also keeps your brain healthy too? Your brain is sometimes called the 'master controller' because of how much influence it has over your body. Your brain also controls how you experience life as it takes in and interprets information – that is what makes your experience unique to everyone else's. Such an important organ is worth protecting, which is why your brain sits safely inside your hard, bony skull. But keeping your brain in your skull is like keeping it in a dark cave, it has to rely on the messages coming from your spinal cord for its information.

Physically moving your spine is vital for keeping your brain alive. Nobel Prize recipient Dr Roger Sperry found that the spine is the motor that drives the brain. According to his research, 90% of stimulation and nutrition to the brain is generated by the movement of the spine. Since your spine is made up of 33 bones, it's important that each one of these can move individually. When motion is lost, a natural process of decline begins. It's called *atrophy*.

Have you ever noticed that when a broken arm or leg is released from its cast, that limb is usually smaller and weaker than its counterpart? Lack of motion even for only 6-8 weeks of being in a cast will cause the muscles to atrophy. The limb will also feel weaker, stiff and painful. However, once the limb is released and starts moving again, the strength naturally returns to the muscle and the joints ease up. Restoring motion to the limb by taking the cast off has allowed it to fully regain its function.

Movement is how your body stays alive. Not just global movements like being able to bend and stretch, but each individual joint needs to move freely in relation to the ones around it. This isn't something that you can easily assess or restore for yourself using stretches which is why most Chiropractors see a colleague to restore the movement in their own spines. While you can choose to start improving your health in any area you choose, I strongly encourage you to get your body moving on both a full-body and spinal level as soon as possible. Movement is a fundamental need for your body and moving it more will make a big impact on your physical and mental health.

HEALTH KEY

90% of the nutrition and stimulation to your brain, comes from movement of the spine

Self-care habit #1: Drink more water

Believe it or not your body is made up of around 70% water – even your teeth are 10% water! Even though some people claim to never drink water and be perfectly fine, water is absolutely essential for your long-term health as it cleans the inside of your body and transports vitamins and minerals to your cells. Science is constantly uncovering how dehydration is contributing to the increase in health problems in our society, but we simply don't make the connection. Dehydration or lack of water can cause you to feel tired, have headaches, constipation, mood swings and poor sexual function. Since your body can't store water, you need to drink throughout the day to stay hydrated.

The feeling of thirst is often confused with hunger or cravings for coffee or alcohol. Hypnotherapist Paul McKenna calls water 'the magic weight loss elixir' and helps people to lose weight simply by first answering pangs of hunger with a large glass of water. Your goal should be to drink 1 litre of water per 30kg of body weight, spread throughout the day. Drink more if you are unwell, or have had coffee or alcohol, both of which can strip your body of water. If you want a simple new habit with big impact, start with this.

Self-care habit #2: Sort your posture

Your mother was doing you a big favour when she told you to "stop slouching!" Bad posture is probably the most common cause of physical trauma to your central nervous system. It has even been linked with developing heart disease and depression. Sitting with your legs crossed is particularly bad for you as it invites twisting and rotation into the pelvis and spine.

Developing good posture begins with becoming aware of your body in space. Always sit with both feet firmly planted on the floor, with your weight spread evenly across both sit-bones. Try to sit with your hips higher than your knees so your weight is slightly forward. This makes it easier for your shoulders to line up over your pelvis and for your back to remain straight. In this posture your body is much more at ease and able to rest. Do the same when you stand, ensuring your weight is equal on both feet and shoulders sit over the pelvis, not hunched forwards. This will feel unnatural in the beginning, however with consistency over time you will come to find that slouching and twisting create discomfort in your spine.

Before good posture feels 'normal', you are likely to experience some aching in the muscles of the back and shoulders as your postural muscles regain their strength. However, it is worth the discomfort as when your body is stacked on an even foundation, it is much easier for it to withstand the test of time. I find it helpful to ask a loved one or workmate to gently prompt when they notice you slouching or twisting. Screen savers, phone prompts and Post-its all make good alternatives if your loved ones take too much pleasure in reminding you!

Self-care habit #3: Make time to rest and play

We live in a culture where being exhausted and busy are seen as status symbols. You have time to rest? You're obviously not working hard enough! Wrong. But given the pressure there is to achieve as much as you can in a day, it takes courage to prioritise rest and play. Regular rest increases healing, productivity and concentration as it allows your body to spend time in a state of ease and restoration. You may feel as though you are 'doing nothing' when you rest, but you are actually making sure that the time you are doing something is more productive AND protecting your health.

Rest is not the same as enjoying a hobby, which usually requires some effort. Rest is where you minimise your physical and mental efforts for at least an hour: relaxing to read a book, sitting in quiet reflection, taking a bath, listening to music or even binge watching your favourite TV show, so long as it requires very little concentration or emotional stress.

Like rest, play is a great source of energy but is more effortful. Play includes activities where you lose track of time, feel free to be yourself and feel uninhibited. Time spent in play doesn't have a specific purpose other than your own enjoyment. Dr Stuart Brown who researched the concept of play, concluded that the opposite of play is not work, the opposite of play is depression. You have a biologically programmed need for play which needs to be indulged regularly to renew your sense of excitement in life.

Make a list of everything you enjoy which makes you rest and make time for it at least once a week for an hour. When it comes to play, get the whole family involved, make a list of everything you all love to do (including the kids) and see where there is some crossover. For us it's Lego, crafting and walking. This is how we spend our family time so everyone can benefit together.

Self-care habit #4: Calm your anxiety

When your body experiences stress, it responds with the fight or flight survival state and you 'fight' the stress with stress releasing behaviours like exercise, adjustments or meditation. When it comes to feelings of anxiety, the worst thing you can do is try to fight it. Anxiety is often a symptom of stress, but it is not the same thing. *Fighting* anxiety reinforces the chemical stress in your body which makes anxiety worse.

Feeling anxious can be a healthy response. For example, if you are driving on a dark, windy road where you can't see properly and feel as though you may crash at any time, you feel anxious and slow down. The feeling of anxiety disappears once you have safely reached your destination.

Unhealthy anxiety happens when you feel unsafe or fearful when you aren't in any specific danger. Many adults and children experience anxiety but they don't know how to deal with it. If this is true for you, then reducing the anxiety in your life is an important step in creating positive changes for your health.

One solution is to practice finding things to feel grateful for, because it is impossible for your brain to feel anxious AND grateful at the same time. This is easier said than done, but it works. Even better, once you get into the groove of finding small, seemingly insignificant things in your life to be grateful for, your subconscious brain will be on the look-out for good things that you can note at the end of each day. After a while, your brain is automatically looking for reasons to feel safe instead of threatened. This technique works even if you simply think of 5 things each day that you feel grateful for. It's even more powerful if you share it with someone or write it down. I know some families who share a gratitude with each other over dinner, it sounds corny but it can give you an interesting insight into the lives of your children!

There is another way to ease anxiety around a specific event, like a child going for a sleepover or you giving a presentation at work. In your body, anxiety feels the same as excitement – your heart beats faster and you have butterflies in your stomach. The only way your brain can tell whether you are anxious or excited is from the word you use to label the feeling. Reminding yourself that you are *excited* to start the new job can help you to re-frame the physical feelings in your mind.

Self-care habit #5: Take deep breaths

There's a reason we tell a child to take a deep breath when they are hurt or in distress. Breathing deeply releases a cascade of chemicals in your brain that allows the fog in your brain to clear and your body to relax. Sometimes you do everything right and still become overwhelmed with stress, anxiety or worry or a difficult situation can arise at work and you feel yourself going into fight or flight mode.

Take a deep breath in and fill your lungs for a count of 2 seconds, then hold it for 2 more seconds before breathing out, until your lungs are completely empty. Repeat this 3 to 4 times until you feel calm. Deep breathing is also important in daily life and not just in emergencies. Engaging your diaphragm (the muscle deep inside your tummy) when you breathe gives your body and brain more oxygen. On the other hand, shallow breathing with the top of your chest reduces the essential oxygen in your body and makes your chest feel tighter. Focussing on breathing deeply when you've just woken up or before going to bed is a wonderful way to re-oxygenate your blood, connect with your body and calm your mind.

Self-care habit #6: Make time to be peaceful

Unlike specific periods of rest, you can make time to be peaceful at any point in your day and experience the benefit, even if you only do it for a few seconds. I have 3 ways of achieving mental peace in my life: mindfulness, meditation and silence.

Mindfulness is about learning to be in the present moment (rather than constantly thinking about something else) and can be a helpful way to calm your nervous system. Mindfulness is a great tool to help us connect with nature and the world around us in a new way. You probably already walk somewhere – to the shops, with the dog or coming home from work. However, if you normally use that as thinking time, or time to listen to music, a podcast or call a friend, you can replace that with mindfulness. A mindful walk means just you, in silence, paying attention to what's around you: what you can hear, smell and see, how the weather feels on your face and how your body feels as it moves. Experiment with how different your mood is when you try a mindful walk, compared to one where you distract yourself with an activity while you're out.

Some people feel resistant to meditation because it can have spiritual connections. Getting in touch with your spirit, however, is incredibly important. That doesn't have to mean God or religion. But taking 10 minutes to sit in silence, on your own and paying attention to whatever thoughts or feelings come up for you is an important form of meditation. Rather than paying attention to what you can smell, hear and feel as you would in mindfulness, the purpose of meditation in this sense is to try to switch off your brain and be in your body.

Both mindfulness and meditation allow you to separate your 'self' from your thoughts. Think of your thoughts as being leaves floating down a stream, or clouds passing through a sky. You are not the leaves or the clouds, you are something bigger. In this larger space you are able to think and feel in new ways, disconnecting from your brain, into your body. Creating a friendly, trusting relationship with your body is the best way to safeguard your health as you begin to notice the feedback from your body when your mind is quiet.

The third way of achieving peace, sitting in silence, is the most recent one I have tried, and quite possibly my favourite. When you have a 'busy brain' that's difficult to shut off, trying to force it to focus on something in a mindful or meditative way can feel difficult. Sitting in silence is just that, setting an alarm for 10 minutes and just being quiet. Nothing specific to focus on just learning how to be. In the beginning your mind will still race, but over time the silence and inactivity in your body begins to slow it down. This peaceful time can quickly become the best part of your day as you embrace nothingness for a change!

Self-care habit #7: Check your sleep routine

Good sleep allows your brain to work better, balances your mood, aids weight loss, maintains balance in the body and lets it repair itself. Sleep increases your energy and your ability to fight disease. There's a reason that sleep deprivation is used as a form of torture! The amount of sleep you need varies, however scientists believe that everyone needs at least 7 hours of sleep per night, even more for children and teenagers.

The best way to make sure you sleep well is to create consistent habits: go to bed and get up at the same time so your body develops a rhythm. It's best if you can stay in your rhythm as much as possible, even on holidays and weekends. We all know that babies and young children need a sleep routine, so their brain and body begin to switch off naturally at night. No matter how old you get, you can always improve your sleep by creating a sleep routine. Do things that relax you before bed like reading, bathing or journaling. The purpose is to get your brain to wind down. This is why emotionally-charged conversations, gaming, TV, working on a laptop and being on the internet should be avoided near bedtime because they increase activity in your brain instead of reducing it. Your sleep space is also important. Light levels, temperature, noise and your surroundings all make a difference to your ability to relax and switch off.

Getting enough sleep is as important to your future health as drinking enough water. Invest in a good mattress and pillow which support your body so it can lie in a neutral position which doesn't put any strain on your spine or neck. Experiment to see what suits you best. Start with basics like cutting out an evening activity you know isn't helping you sleep, like checking your mobile phone in bed, or try sticking to the same bedtime every night for a month.

Self-care habit #8: Filter the modern world

We live a world which is more connected through technology than ever before. While this has many advantages, it also has disadvantages to your physical and mental health. Time spent on screens is bad for your posture, changes the way your brain works and can stop you connecting with friends and family in the real world. In a presentation given by a children's mental health specialist, he described giving our children free access to the internet as "like asking them to gulp water through a garden hose." Technology and the internet are wonderful opportunities for our children and ourselves to connect, work and learn, but it can quickly become overwhelming.

You can enjoy the benefits of the modern world while still protecting your health when you become conscious about how you engage with technology. Try to be aware of when it is useful to you, and consciously turn it off when it isn't. This can mean going for a walk without music or your phone and turning your phone off for periods in the day so you don't feel constantly contactable, or compelled to scroll mindlessly. Have you experienced that feeling of release when you can't get a phone signal on a remote holiday? Recreate it for yourself at home.

I also recommend filtering the kind of TV you and your family watch. Entertainment has become about putting the viewer on an emotional rollercoaster with never-ending shocks, scares or sadness to keep us engaged. This is fine from time to time, however the kind of stress represented on our British soaps for example, creates that same stress in our bodies. Constantly negative or upsetting news reports can also leave you feeling depressed all day. Becoming aware of what you are watching and reading and the effect it has on your own emotions is a powerful way of reducing unnecessary stress in your life. Choose to watch a comedy programme or even better set a household time for all the technology to be off. After all, being bored is what leads to creativity!

Self-care habit #9: Start eating mindfully

Have you ever sat in front of a movie and consumed an entire bag of crisps or sweets before glanced down surprised that they have all gone? This mechanical, distracted way of consuming food is the opposite of mindful eating. There is a hormone called 'leptin' which is released by your fat cells to signal to your brain that you are full. Throughout my life I've been surprised by people who say, "I couldn't possibly eat another bite" because I could always have another bite! I have come to realise that my brain is probably not overly sensitive to leptin and that I need to pay close attention to when I feel full. For me it is a tiny nudge and not a firm signal. Regardless of how easy it is for you to feel full, eating mindfully is important as it prevents overeating and allows you to enjoy every mouthful.

Eating mindfully means several things: eating sitting at a table with no distractions (no TV, phones or books), chewing every bite slowly before swallowing and paying attention for that signal that you are becoming full. You will also start to notice that your food tastes less good as you become satisfied. Challenge yourself to take at least 20 minutes to eat your meal and notice what a difference it makes to your eating habits.

Mindful eating can also be an important part of discovering the types of food that work best for your body. This is how I came to realise that my body prefers a vegetarian diet. Have you ever eaten something sweet and tasty and noticed it wasn't as satisfying as you expected? Usually that's because you answered the call of hunger with the wrong food. In pregnancy the body as unusual hunger cravings for elements or minerals it needs to build the baby. The natural intelligence in your body will tell you what you need if only you know how to hear it!

Self-care habit #10: Do a lifestyle assessment

The purpose behind self-care is for you to get to know yourself better, so that ultimately you can create the future you want to experience. This means becoming accountable for your own health and the only way to do this effectively is to regularly assess your lifestyle.

If you are someone who likes to collect data you might want to keep a note of various factors you are interested in monitoring: body weight, Body Mass Index, water intake, Basal Metabolic Rate, a sleep diary. You can go online and fill out lots of information to get more data to help you assess your health. There are lots of apps to help you track your sleep and even your stress levels by monitoring your heart rate variability. How deep you want to go is entirely your choice.

A simpler solution would be to use your wheel of health and regularly review it to re-focus your attention in different areas. You can make a list of easy changes you would like to implement over the next 6 months and keep returning to it. Whatever approach works for you – the most important thing is that you do continue to assess and re-assess your lifestyle in a way that is meaningful to you.

Do Try This at Home

Just as every part of your body affects every other part, you are also affected by everyone you live with. Your family are a large part of your emotional environment. There are useful ways that you can generally reduce the stress levels in your whole household when you need to. When it comes to your family unit, you should look at the same areas you would in your own life.

For example, is everyone eating nourishing food? Prioritising fresh, home-cooked food and avoiding sugary or processed food will stabilise the energy levels of the household. Creating a bedtime routine for everyone in the family, where everyone goes to bed at a consistent time each night (suited to their age, not at the same time) will give everyone better sleep, focus and more energy. Support each other with better bedtime routines of washing, reading and relaxing before bed. If one member really struggles in this area, it will help them to know everyone is following the same routine.

Turning down the general noise in the house will help calm everyone's nervous system. This can mean having agreed quiet times, or times when technology is turned off. It can also be as easy as lowering the volume of any TVs, computers and music to create a calmer atmosphere. Turning down bright lights will also help, alongside having periods without machine noise (games consoles, hoovers, washing machines) and try seeing what it's like to only hear each other! Remember that time for play and rest are important for everyone in the family.

In practical terms there is a simple massage technique you can also use to 'de-amplify' or calm the nervous system. I like to ask the youngest child to be in charge of making sure everybody does this at home. This is a massage that you can do for yourself, or do for someone else and it activates the deep touch pathways of the body and creates a feeling of safety and calm, just like when you swaddle a new born baby. Begin by squeezing both sides of your face with wide open palms, moving down to the neck, chest, torso, thighs, knees and calves, all the way down the body.

Repeat at least 3 times or until you feel fully relaxed and calm.

> HEALTH KEY
>
> A balanced nervous system isn't just important for the individual, but also for the entire family

What will your journey look like?

When I we made the big move to Edinburgh, my husband and I fell in love with an ugly house with the most amazing view of the Pentland hills. I adore watching them in a kaleidoscope of colour as the weather changes almost hourly. It makes me feel so happy and connected to nature. The week we moved in, a huge white tarpaulin bag got left right in the middle of the garden and I never bothered to move it.

One morning I woke up to the most spectacular rainbow appearing from behind a tree in the garden, arching over the Pentlands in perfect form. This was exactly why we had chosen to upend our lives for this house, and I wanted to share the image with my friends. The only thing spoiling that otherwise perfect photograph was the giant white bag slap bang in the middle of it.

There may not be a great big health problem looming for you right now but I am sure there are a few habits which, like the tarpaulin bag, interrupt the beautiful landscape of your life. By choosing to act now, you not only save yourself problems in the future, but maximise your enjoyment of today. By incorporating healthy habits into your life, you are not only increasing your ability to deal with stress as it happens and creating a strong nervous system that will help you recover if you become sick, but hopefully adding many happy years to your life. These valuable changes cannot be rushed, there is no shortcut to bypass the work. The fastest way you can create change is to build more positive habits on top of each other over time and keep going.

Health is a journey with many ups and downs and healing is rarely simple or straightforward. Because of this you will also benefit from the help of health professionals along the way. Whichever areas of your life you choose to focus on for your health goals, you can improve your likelihood of success threefold when you seek the help of an expert in that area. Pick someone you trust and like, follow their advice consistently and give your body time to change. About 12 months is a realistic timeframe to allow the approach to work for your body in a lasting and meaningful way.

If you find you haven't managed to meet your target this is usually because you expected too much of yourself, you didn't allow enough time, or you didn't ask for support or expertise when you needed it. Not to worry, re-set the goal and try again. My hope is by reading this book you now have a much clearer understanding of how the internal and external factors of your life affect your health and what you can do about it. You can make many of these changes for free simply by being motivated and informed, and even more when you get support from others.

Above all things, I believe your future health and success depends on building a strong relationship with your body, honouring how it is made and how your life choices affect it. When you learn to trust in your own natural intelligence and intuition, you can step away from the fear and uncertainty we experience in modern life, and retreat to the calm and confident place within. It's a sanctuary that once found, no one can take away: health and happiness from the top, down, inside, out. I hope you find your path towards a thriving life spent in ease and fulfilment and that this book has helped you take the next right step.

The key to the life you want lies within you: you are the answer.

About the Author

Naomi Mills is a family Chiropractor, mother, teacher and author. She is passionate about creating change in how we see health and ourselves

Naomi has worked in some form of healthcare for the last 20 years, half in traditional medicine and half in natural healthcare. She has always loved working with people but found our traditional model of healthcare didn't quite fit her because it focuses almost exclusively on when things go wrong with your body rather than how our bodies are naturally clever and designed to heal themselves given the right environment.

In 2011, she graduated as a Doctor of Chiropractic from the Anglo-European College of Chiropractic and began experiencing first-hand how having a healthy nervous system can change people's lives. She spent the first 10 years of her career running a busy family Chiropractic centre in Nottingham before feeling called back to her native Scotland. She lives on the outskirts of Edinburgh with her husband Richard, daughter Beatrix and dogs Jelly and Frank.

Naomi spends her time at Life and Light Chiropractic, mentoring other Chiropractors and teaching locally. Her spare time is spent with family, crafting, reading, walking, meditating and connecting with friends.